MADE IN NORWAY

NORWEGIAN ARCHITECTURE TODAY

IMPRINT

Edited by:
Arkitektur N, the Norwegian Review of Architecture
Josefines gate 34
NO-0351 Oslo
Norway
www.arkitektur-n.no

Arkitektur N is published by
the National Association of Norwegian Architects
www.arkitektur.no

Editor-in-chief: Ingerid Helsing Almaas
Editors: Einar Bjarki Malmquist, Åsne Maria Gundersen,
Helle Benedicte Berg
Project coordinator: Helle Benedicte Berg
Design: Janne Solvang
Layout: Gro Otterstad

English translations: Alison Philip, Richard Lawson, Ingerid
Helsing Almaas, Helle Benedicte Berg, Vibecke Dixon and
Pete Dixon.

Excerpts from poems by Tone Hødnebø and Tor Ulven:
Tor Ulven: *Samlede dikt* (ed. Morten Moi), Gyldendal 2000
Tone Hødnebø: *Stormstigen*, Kolon 2002
English translations by Ingerid Helsing Almaas

Print: Fix Repro, Oslo, Norway
Font: Futura/Scala
Paper: Galerie Art Silk

Produced with the generous support of the Norwegian Ministry of Foreign Affairs

Cover: Gudbrandsjuvet landscape hotel. Architects: Jensen &
Skodvin Arkitektkontor. Photo: Jensen & Skodvin

NORWEGIAN MINISTRY
OF FOREIGN AFFAIRS

MADE IN NORWAY

NORWEGIAN ARCHITECTURE TODAY

INGERID HELSING ALMAAS (ED.)

ARKITEKTUR N

BIRKHÄUSER

CONTENTS

Architecture today

Does "Made in Norway" actually have any meaning today in visual terms? How can we define what is distinctively Norwegian?

Surely trends in architecture and design know no national borders. Today's world is – more than anything else – characterised by a fine network of interconnected events and trends that affect each other across national borders. Therefore, today we talk about the meeting of different cultures, cultural exchanges and, not least, about the mutual dependence that ties together the nations of a globalised world, which may be greater now than ever before in human history.

In this situation, where decisions made in faraway places or in one of the many international cooperation bodies may have a bigger impact on our everyday life than decisions made at home, we might think that the role of the nation state has been weakened.

But in fact, the opposite may well be true, and the field of architecture is a case in point. Despite the globalisation of the building industry during the last century, architecture – perhaps more than many other fields of human endeavour – has to respond to local conditions – such as the weather. Providing shelter for human activities is still the primary purpose of most of our buildings, and the challenges posed by different climates will continue to shape architecture in different ways. Cold climates will rarely produce the same architecture as warmer ones.

But architecture is, of course, also a cultural response. Architecture is never based on a single truth; it is never a fixed answer to a given set of conditions. Design involves making choices, and in those choices our natural, social and economic resources are transformed into an expression of our culture, which offers new possibilities. Buildings reflect the ideas, values and priorities of a society. Through our architecture, we demonstrate who we are, both as individuals and as a community.

The projects in this book are examples of how Norwegian clients, architects and builders have responded to different situations in Norway today. They address various challenges posed by contemporary Norwegian society: How do we develop our cities? How do we deal with history? How do we create spaces where people can meet and interact in ways that are relevant and productive today? And, not least, how do we respond to the natural landscape?

This last question has perhaps given Norwegian architecture one of its distinctive characteristics. Norway is sparsely populated outside the main cities. It is a coastal nation where the sea, fjords, mountains and forests are never far away, and the relationship to the untouched natural landscape continues to be an important feature of many of our building projects. It has been said that our buildings are close to nature, and subjected to powerful natural forces, but our best architecture provides a challenge or a contrast that allows for a deeper understanding of both nature and culture.

Norwegian architecture has attracted international attention during the last couple of decades, culminating in several prestigious international awards, such as the Pritzker Prize to Sverre Fehn in 1997, and last year's Mies van der Rohe award to Snøhetta for the Opera House in Oslo. Despite its small population, Norway has the potential to make an important contribution to design and architecture, particularly in those areas where Norway is at the forefront internationally, such as social welfare, responsible management of natural resources and sustainable development.

Architecture is a globalised field where a single nation can produce something distinctive and unique that will be of value to the international community. The projects in this book are examples of this.

Oslo, March 2010

Jonas Gahr Støre

Jonas Gahr Støre
MINISTER OF FOREIGN AFFAIRS

Facing page: Oslo Opera House. Snøhetta 2009.
PHOTO: HELENE BINET

A new sense of place

The connection between place and identity have been a source of great inspiration for architects for most of the last half of the 20th century. Architectural historians and theorists have summed this interest up in different ways. The late Christian Norberg-Schulz contributed his well-known speculations concerning the spirit of place, the genius loci, and Kenneth Frampton introduced a discourse on the term "critical regionalism", a term also rooted in an understanding of local conditions as the source of meaning in architecture.

Obviously, an understanding of local conditions, and the details of those conditions, is central to creating architecture anywhere. But this focus has a flipside: Whilst tying identity, be it personal or national identity, to a particular sense of place might make sense in terms of architecture, it is actually deeply problematic on a social and political level. The problem arises when our understanding of what constitutes the local conditions for building is no longer dynamic, but becomes fixed to certain interpretations or forms. If we connect the qualities of a certain place with our perception of identity, personal or national, we also inevitably start to create boundaries: Identity becomes fixed and exclusive. Life becomes static.

The moment the question of who you are is answered with reference to where you come from, as in "I am a Norwegian", it gives you a connection to other people who are from the same place, but it also sets you apart from people who are from other places. Contemporary Norway has been largely protected from the most extreme consequences of this problem for a couple of generations, but you don't have to look very far outside our borders before you see all to clearly the tragic consequences of the close associations of identity and place. Former Yugoslavia, for example, where thousands of people were killed in the early 1990's because they came from the wrong place, or came from the right place, but were in the wrong place. As soon as who you are is tied to where

you are, or where you come from, you come dangerously close to erecting unscalable barriers between people. The world is changing. A billion people are on the move around the world. If we tie identity primarily to place, we rob these people of their identities.

Architects have a particular responsibility in relation to this very complex problem. The very general idea that architecture reflects human life is central in all our work in one way or another. And if people cannot see themselves in their surroundings, then what will give meaning to architecture? If a sense of place depends on recognizing something you already know, how can we make an architecture that has meaning to people with completely different lives and memories? Obviously, the specific preconditions of a place remains as a reference when we build: The climate makes its specific demands, the programme for the building will reflect the specifics of the social circumstances, certain building materials and types of construction will be more readily available than others. So, in order to create a meaningful architecture for a globalised world, the answer must be to look beyond these specifics, or, rather, to look deeper into the specifics of an architectural response, to find something of universal value.

Most people know very little about Norway. There are, after all, only about 4,8 million Norwegians, a miniscule proportion of the world's population. The likelihood of meeting a Norwegian, even on the streets of some of the biggest cities in the world, is very slight. However, perhaps precisely because the world knows only little of Norwegians and Norwegian architecture, we have all the more opportunity to make an impact, if only through the element of surprise. Very few people know our references, very few people have been to the places that we might think meaningful, and therefore, to most people, our architecture will be free of associations, ready to be interpreted in new and foreign ways. The people confronted with, for

example, the projects in this book, will see these pictures with fresh eyes, and so have the potential to awaken new associations – beyond what was intended by the architects who designed the buildings, or the photographers who took the pictures, or the writers of the texts.

And only those who are strangers to the context of Norwegian architecture will have this gift of fresh sight, of new interpretations. In a world where the stranger is often met with suspicion, this may be a timely reminder: There are many ways to meet what we have never seen before. We can reject it; or we can look for the familiar and thereby absorb the new with indifference, or we can meet it with a curiosity that might even grow into admiration. Admiration can have a profound impact on our identity. Admiration is the reaction we get when we see something that is obviously excellent, and we think: "I really wish I'd done that". We remember and carry with us parts of what we have seen, and in a way, when we see the best of other people's work, we see in the excellence of someone else's achievements the possibility of excellence in ourselves, pregnant with future possibilities, possible future identities. Admiration is the antidote to exclusivity, self-absorption, to national chauvinism. This is the promise of a globalised world: The opportunity to admire the excellence of others.

Ingerid Helsing Almaas

EDITOR, ARKITEKTUR N

Above: Architecture reflects human life. Fantastic Norway and their red camper van at the Venice Architecture Biennale 2008.

PHOTO: IHA

A reflection of a Norwegian identity? Passive energy houses, Tromsø, by Steinsvik Arkitektkontor. View from the roof terrace.
PHOTO: RAVN STEINSVIK

THE STATE OF IDENTITY IN CONTEMPORARY ARCHITECTURE

Where are you actually from? In a globalised world, where more and more people move around and continuously have to renew their ties with their environment, the idea of "place" as a source of individual or national identity has to be reconsidered.

ESSAY | **HANS SKOTTE**
Associate Professor, Norwegian University of Science and Technology

Much of the Norwegian architecture debate during the last three decades of the 20th century circled around the concept of *Genius Loci* – the spirit of place. The Norwegian architectural theorist Christian Norberg-Schulz was one of those who, during the 1980s, put forward the notion of endemicity as perhaps the most important of architectural principles. Architecture was defined as a form of "Place Art". But this concept is fundamentally problematic in a world where nearly a billion people are migrants or long-term commuters across national borders and many more move to places far from where they once grew up. What does this entail for the identity of a location – and for the architecture built there?

Architects work within a discipline where the development of practice has not been dependent on theoretical innovations. To take an extreme view, what we architects have formulated, from Roman times to the present, have either been time dependent "design postulates" or interpretations and adaptations of theories from different disciplines. These sparse formulations nonetheless constitute the maps of our discipline. The question is, then, whether the maps provided by Norberg-Schulz are of any help to our navigation?

In the following, I will approach this question from a practical rather than a theoretical angle. The grand Theories of Place must be reformulated by others. My small contribution is based on reflections grounded in having worked abroad as well as experience and studies of reconstruction after war and disasters. The latter is important as underlying ideologies – including architectural ideologies – seem to become more visible in such extreme situations. This primarily applies to the notion that one's identity is inextricably bound to and formed by a specific territory, language and religion, which we refer to as a notion of "primordial ethnicity". Norberg-Schulz's Genius Loci-concept may seem to lie dangerously close to such fundamentalist spheres of thought. "Identity architecture" may thus easily become a hazardous project. For instance, for me personally, no "Norwegian" architecture exists other than buildings erected in Norway. And moreover – and here lies the primordialist stumbling block – *Norwegian architecture is not dependent on the architect being Norwegian.* By analogy, what we refer to as Le Corbusier's Chandigarh complex has actually become part of the Indian architectural heritage, as is Mughal architecture.

The latter was also 'inflicted' upon India at one time.

National identity – architecture as a tool of reconstruction
Architecture has always been used to express power. However, through the emergence of the European nation states and democracy in the nineteenth century, architects were charged with new major cultural policy tasks. They were to design "national environments", create national symbols.[1] And everywhere, in all countries, the source of this was sought in the countryside, where time stood still – that's where the primordial models were to be found.[2]

This is how Norway went about the search for ideals for our own reconstruction architecture after World War II. As early as the autumn of 1940, the catalogue *Norwegian Houses for Town and Country* was presented. The models presented here were to ensure that the buildings erected to replace those destroyed by the Germans "satisfied the requirement that sound building practices and modern design be associated with rural building traditions", as was stated by the Reconstruction Board of the Office for War Damage.[3] In other words, it was of crucial importance that what was to be rebuilt should be "Norwegian".

"A NATION'S IDENTITY CANNOT BE CAPTURED IN FRESH TIMBER AND WET CONCRETE."

All the more so since that was the reason for their destruction. The field of architecture was thereby assigned an autonomous national reconstruction task. The awarded entries in the architectural competition for post-war houses in 1945 were all wooden buildings with sparse detailing, with functional layouts, all carrying an air of simplicity and neatness. This was how architects interpreted "the Norwegian" in contemporary housing architecture. However, later research indicates that the families occupying these "competition houses", at any rate in the far north, had a different perception of these houses. Neither in their orientation nor in their layout did they reflect the lifestyle of the local farmer-fishermen. Of the 20 000 dwellings (12 000 in the far north) destroyed during the war, only 638 were replaced by "competition houses", and no more of them were built after 1947. The architects' concrete interpretations of "the Norwegian" seemed to indicate a cultivated and possibly distorted view of history. This would not, as such, have been a specifically Norwegian phenomenon. Everywhere where reconstruction after disasters and war is on the agenda there seems to be a general call for return to an idealized "original state". The UN *Guidelines on Shelter after Natural Disasters* (UNDRO 1982) point out the danger of relying solely on architects in reconstruction planning, because they often introduce urban middle-class ideals that are inappropriate for victims in rural areas. We have observed this for example in post-tsunami Sri Lanka. The first thing that the devastated families did after receiving the standardised donor houses, largely designed by local architects, was to erect primitive extensions made of box board and corrugated iron, because the layout of the houses did not enable the families to live as they were accustomed to. They needed other types of rooms, especially for making food and for personal hygiene. The orientation and floor plan of the houses also often failed to comply with prevalent traditions. This happened in spite of the national rhetoric claiming that the physical reconstruction also was to be a cultural reconstruction.

In both Norway and Sri Lanka, the nationalist charge of the reconstruction was the result of a preceding international or ongoing national conflict. In both cases the architects' task was to strengthen national identity. However, in neither case did they succeed in accomplishing this objective. This was perhaps not so strange; the objective was illusive. A nation's identity cannot be captured in fresh timber and wet concrete.

National identity – architecture as an instrument of development
African independence in the 1960's was accompanied by similar architectural challenges. Independence and national pride needed literally to be built from scratch. This required consultants and contractors. During the 1960's and into the 1970's, the continent was therefore inundated with foreign experts charged with constructing buildings signalling national identity. Norway's Karl Henrik Nøstvik was responsible for one of the most prominent of these projects. He was the architect for the Kanu Party's headquarters and the Kenyatta Internatio-

"EVEN THE SMALLEST ONE-ROOM HEALTH CENTRES WERE EXPECTED TO HAVE FOUR CORNERS, BE BUILT OF BRICK, HAVE CORRUGATED IRON ROOFS AND BE PAINTED WHITE."

nal Conference Centre in Nairobi, Kenya. As the headquarters of the country's only political party at the time, it was naturally Kenya's tallest building, and it was duly crowned by a gigantic traditional straw-roof shape. Similar buildings signifying progress were erected in other African countries. For example, Norwegian consultants were closely involved in the design of secondary schools in Zambia. The design of these buildings adopted a technology so removed from what people were familiar with, that some decades later they literally almost fell apart – and were on the point of dragging the whole secondary school system with them. But progress demanded its formal expression.

When I myself began working in Africa in the mid 1980's, the prevalent local perception of the traditional building forms was that they totally lacked the capacity to house "development activities". Even the smallest one-room health centres were expected to have four corners, be built of brick, have corrugated iron roofs and be painted white. The local perception of development was in other words associated with imported building forms.

This has always been the case. The Nidaros Cathedral in Trondheim, a romanesque soapstone edifice from the 12th century, is Norway's foremost example of an imported building form. There were originally almost no Norwegian input to the building other than the stone, the timber and the lay workers. But herein lies perhaps the germ of an solution to the predicament.

Architectural ecology
Because, it is not a matter of the forms themselves, but of how they are created in the given conditions. The Indian architect Charles Correa likens identity to the trail left by civilisation as it moves through history. That which is distinctive is thus that which emerges *subsequent to* an ongoing process. Consequently, it cannot be collectively programmed. The concept of identity is by nature reflexive, that is to say self-regulating, and it is creative.

Architecture is located in a field determined by the economic, material, technological and social resources of a location.[4] Here, there are no primordial quantities. Everything is in reciprocal motion. However, behind us lies Correa's trail. Here lie traditions like a kind of developmental inertia, a historical flywheel that ensures continuity and a certain predictability. It is in this unstable ecological field that the architect works. This inertia provides us with references to methods that are still meaningful, to details and materials, to space and spatial expression and to modes of action. All of this is tested against innovations, including architectural innovations. Such an approach is liberating in the sense that it departs from the deterministic, xenophobic concept of a pre-defined identity, and releases architects from a nationalist commitment. This allows the Norwegian architects Jan Olav Jensen and Per Christian Brynildsen to be inspired by Indian architecture in the construction of a Lepers' Hospital in India, and gives Hans Olav Hesselberg and Sixten Rahlff the opportunity to include elements from the Nepalese architectural tradition in their Children's Home in Chebettar.[5] And what about Snøhetta's contribution to Egyptian architecture with the new Library of Alexandria, and Henning Larsen's contribution to Norwegian building tradition through a number of important projects in Norway? In a similar way, Ken Yeang, not least through the Menara Mesiniaga building in Kuala Lumpur, has contributed to a renewal of Malaysian architecture, indeed to a redefinition of the very term skyskraper. Contemporary technology is not used here to "renew" old building forms. Taking his starting point in urban reality and local climate conditions, Yeang has combined established technology and ecological insight to pro-

The Spirit of place? The Wilondja family in front of their house in Vadsø, northern Norway.

A step on Correa's path. Jean-Marie Tjibaou Cultural Centre, New Caledonia. Renzo Piano Building Workshop, 1998.

"THE INDIAN ARCHITECT CHARLES CORREA LIKENS IDENTITY TO THE TRAIL LEFT BY CIVILISATION AS IT MOVES THROUGH HISTORY."

vide form and content to a new, locally adapted architecture.

Equally radical, yet inextricably associated with Correa's trail is the new Tjibaou Culture Centre in Noumea, New Caledonia, designed by the Renzo Piano Building Workshop. Given that this building succeeds in capturing the dynamics of the historical flywheel also in its content, it stands for me as the very epitome of locally adapted architecture. The material references are obvious, but the forms are new, and the building process itself and the social activities that the building is designed for are able to contribute to a form of *"global"* development that I personally view as very positive. For me, the culture centre manifests itself as a New Caledonian version of the Nidaros Cathedral. In a few years' time, it is unlikely that anyone will be preoccupied with the fact that the architect was Italian. The building will have become part of the New Caledonian trail of culture.

Hans Skotte

Hans Skotte is Associate Professor at the Department of Urban Design and Planning at the Norwegian University of Science and Technology in Trondheim.

NOTES

1 In Norway during the 1850s, "Have nation – need culture!" was the culture policy revival message that rang out across the land. From Berggren, Brit (1989): *Da kulturen kom til Norge* [When Culture Came to Norway]. Oslo : Aschehoug.

2 "Folkearkitekturen er stedskunstens opphav. Den er svaret på å skulle bo *her*" ["The origin of Place Art is rural architecture. It provides the answer for living just here"]. Fra Norberg-Schulz, C. (1995): *Stedskunst*. Oslo : Gyldendal.

3 Fra Hage, I (1996): *Som fugl Fønix av asken?* [As the Phoenix out of the ashes?]. Doctoral dissertation, University of Tromsø.

4 In terms of development theory, we may rather have expressed this "in the area of tension between societal capitals ", i.e. between what people are capable of doing by virtue of a) their knowledge and health, b) their financial capital, c) the strength of their social institutions, i.e. the extent of their mutual trust, d) the available natural resources and e) the scope and quality of tools and of the man-made environment.

5 Brynildsen and Jensen received the Aga Khan Architecture Award for their leprosy hospital in India in 1998 and Hesselberg & Rahlff with Synnevåg received both the Ralph Erskine Award and the ar+d award for their school in Nepal. However, in Norway, the buildings have been given the status of 'Norwegian' constructions. Cf. for example the international presentation of Norwegian Contemporary Architecture 1995–2000 by the National Association of Norwegian Architects and the Norwegian Ministry of Foreign Affairs.

Photo credits:
This page: Wilondja family: From Henrik Saxgren *Krig og Kærlighed* (*War and Love*), Gyldendal, Copenhagen 2006.

...

We walked backwards into the future
and no one understood what we said
and we leapt through the centuries
but no one heard if we were approaching
or withdrawing

...

Tone Hødnebø

THE CHALLENGE OF **HISTORY**

Architecture is a very clear expression of our relationship with history. How do we maintain and develop the structures and traditions passed on from previous generations, and how do new ideas form from an understanding of our existing environments? The history of Norway stretches from a poor, rural past through the 18th century monuments of a fledgling nation to today's welfare society.

01 FARM AT SØRUM STANGE

ARE VESTERLID

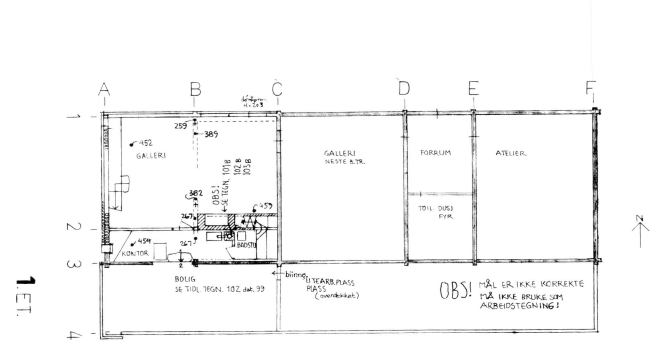

Ground floor plan, converted barn.

An experienced architect and his client, a sculptor, have added a new layer to the building history of an old farmstead.

The farm, which dates back to the 18th century, is now owned by the Norwegian sculptor Knut Wold, who bought it in the mid-1980s. Situated near the town of Hamar, it lies in an open landscape under a wide sky, and looks onto Lake Mjøsa and the Skreiafjellene mountains.

Wold's aim was to restore the buildings by preserving the distinctive features while at the same time being able to use them in new ways. The first step was to build a studio, an office, a shower and a toilet in the barn. Roof lights were instal-led and various small alterations were made. Two arched door-ways from the days when the barn was used for threshing were removed and replaced by windows. In 1999, the architect Are Vesterlid was engaged in the project, and the south-west corner of the barn was renovated as living quarters: a living room with a kitchen measuring about 3.6 m x 9 m, and an open mezza-nine under the 4.3-metre ceiling. The farmyard entrance went through the future gallery space, with a side entrance from a covered outdoor workshop. The existing bathroom was used for the time being. In 2001 the brew house was also renovated as living quarters. In 2003 the loft in the main building was renovated as a studio–living quarters with an outside staircase leading directly up from the farmyard. In 2005 this project was begun: the renovation of the western part of the barn as an art gallery and an addition to the existing living quarters.

"This is not the first time the Sørum farm buildings have been altered," explains the architect. "You can see that the buildings have been shaped by the day-to-day lives of succee-ding generations, by the different uses to which they were put, by being developed, rebuilt and added to, by repair and renova-tion. The main building, which is a fairly simple 18th-century farmhouse, was extended several times, and then during the 1920s a completely foreign architectural style was introduced in the shape of a taller building with a cruciform plan, built at an angle to the old house. Although the old and the new build-ings had a common roof and the same type of cladding, they no longer belonged to any particular architectural style. If that was the point... Perhaps the owner faced the same dilemma as we do today: pull down and rebuild or preserve and add on, and in the latter case: adapt the existing building or make room for contemporary design."

Are Vesterlid

PROJECT INFORMATION: Farm at Sørum, conversion of parts of existing barn. **Address:** Stange. **Client:** Knut Wold, sculptor. **Architect:** Are Vesterlid architect MNAL. **Consultant:** Finn-Erik Nilsen, building engineer. **Gross area of conversion:** 160 sq.m., (total area of the barn: 300 sq.m.). **Photos:** Richard Riesenfeld

ENVIRONMENTAL INFORMATION: Energy sources: Firewood and ground water heat exchange. Large woodburner centrally located in the entrancehall; pipe heats up the living spaces, duct provides additional heating of the gallery area; underfloor heating in concrete slab in the gallery for planned ground water heating. Ventilation: Natural.

NATIONAL MUSEUM – ARCHITECTURE OSLO

SVERRE FEHN

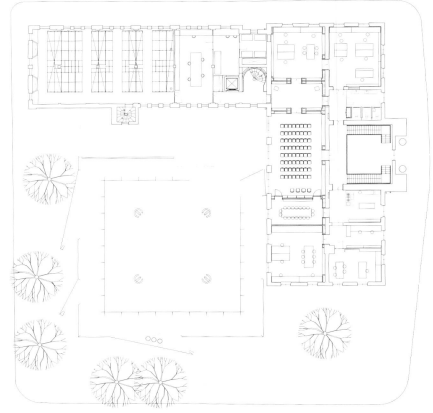

Ground floor plan.

Careful consideration of the existing buildings and the historic urban environment was a key factor for Sverre Fehn in work on the new Norwegian museum of architecture.

Oslo's new museum of architecture, a branch of the National Museum of Art, Architecture and Design, has taken over the oldest premises of the Norwegian Central Bank, designed by Christian Grosch and completed in 1830 as one of Norway's first monumental buildings in the Empire (Regency) style. Sverre Fehn was the architect for both the refurbishment of the old building and the new exhibition pavilion.

The aim of the refurbishment was to recreate the original character of the buildings while accentuating the structure in the interaction with new elements and spaces. All undesirable modern additions have been removed. The original spatial dimensions and features have been partly restored, adapted and refined, and the façades of the main building have been restored to their original appearance.

The idea behind the pavilion was to create an introverted situation, where daylight, the view of the sky and the surrounding environment all play an important role in the experience of the space. The ground plan is a square, with four massive pillars bearing a delicate shell-shaped roof of light concrete. The façades are of glass, and form a thin layer between outdoor and indoor areas. The pavilion is surrounded by external concrete walls, which extend the sense of space, and give the exhibitions a muted backdrop. Throughout the project, a restrained palette of materials is employed. Tile, white pine, lime plaster. Fittings and new building elements are primarily of oak, glass, marble and stainless steel. The pavilion is constructed of light in-situ concrete.

Access to the museum is through the original building. The main entrance leads in to the functions for the general public, such as the lobby with the reception, bookshop, café and exhibition rooms. Temporary exhibitions are shown in the pavilion, while the museum's permanent collection will be housed in the former repository building. To the south, there is access to the park, where there is outdoor catering during the summer months. The museum's administration, library and assembly rooms are on the first floor. The two top floors of the repository building are used as archives for photography and drawing collections and for registration.

Martin Dietrichson

PROJECT INFORMATION: National Museum – Architecture.
Address: Bankplassen 3, Oslo. **Client:** Statsbygg – Public Construction and Property Management. **Architect:** Sverre Fehn
Team: Sverre Fehn, Martin Dietrichson (project manager), Marius Mowé, Kristoffer Moe Bøksle and Henrik Hille (outline project).
Photos: Ivan Brodey.

ENVIRONMENTAL INFORMATION: Estimated energy consumption: Approx. 265 kWh/sq.m./year. **U-values:** The new building has glass façades with a U-value of 1.1 W/sq.m. K. **Energy sources:** Water-borne systems based on district heating. **Ventilation:** Balanced ventilation.

03 | KNUT HAMSUN CENTRE HAMARØY

STEVEN HOLL ARCHITECTS/LY ARKITEKTER

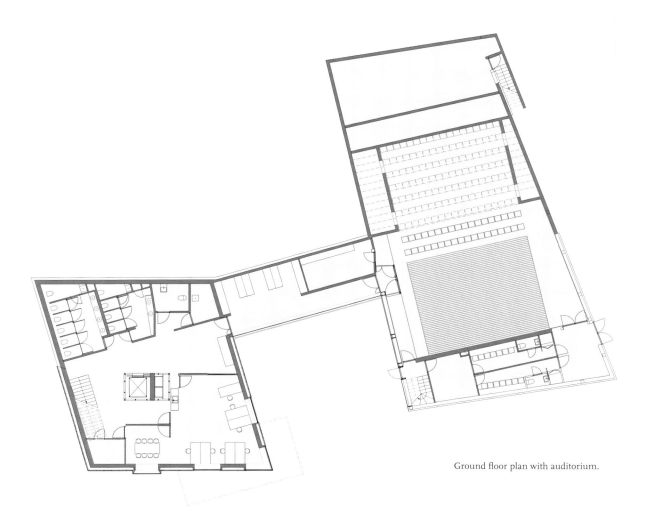

Ground floor plan with auditorium.

The idea behind the Knut Hamsun Centre is based on new interpretations of both the work of the author and aspects of Norwegian building tradition.

Knut Hamsun, Norway's most inventive 20th-century writer, created new forms of expression in his first novel, *Hunger*. He went on to found a truly modern school of fiction with his works *Pan*, *Mysteries*, and *Growth of the Soil*.

This centre dedicated to Hamsun is located above the Arctic Circle near the village of Presteid on Hamarøy near the farm where the writer grew up. The 2300 sq.m. centre includes exhibition areas, a library and reading room, a café, and an auditorium. The building is conceived as an archetypal and intensified compression of spirit in space and light, concretizing a Hamsun character in architectonic terms. The concept for the museum, "Building as a Body: Battleground of Invisible Forces," is realized both inside and outside. Here, the wood exterior is punctuated by hidden impulses piercing through

the surface: An "empty violin case"-balcony has phenomenal sound properties, while a viewing balcony is like the "girl with her sleeves rolled up polishing yellow panes." Many other aspects of the building use the vernacular style as inspiration for reinterpretation. The stained black wood exterior skin is characteristic of the great Norwegian stave churches. On the roof garden, long grass alludes to traditional Norwegian sod roofs in a modern way. The rough white-painted concrete interiors are characterized by diagonal rays of light calculated to ricochet through the section on certain days of the year. These strange, surprising, and phenomenal experiences in space, perspective and light provide an inspiring frame for exhibitions.

Steven Holl

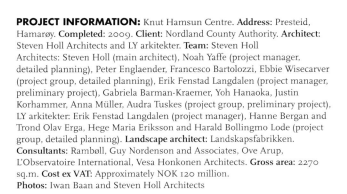

PROJECT INFORMATION: Knut Hamsun Centre. **Address:** Presteid, Hamarøy. **Completed:** 2009. **Client:** Nordland County Authority. **Architect:** Steven Holl Architects and LY arkitekter. **Team:** Steven Holl Architects: Steven Holl (main architect), Noah Yaffe (project manager, detailed planning), Peter Englaender, Francesco Bartolozzi, Ebbie Wisecarver (project group, detailed planning), Erik Fenstad Langdalen (project manager, preliminary project), Gabriela Barman-Kraemer, Yoh Hanaoka, Justin Korhammer, Anna Müller, Audra Tuskes (project group, preliminary project), LY arkitekter: Erik Fenstad Langdalen (project manager), Hanne Bergan and Trond Olav Erga, Hege Maria Eriksson and Harald Bollingmo Lode (project group, detailed planning). **Landscape architect:** Landskapsfabrikken. **Consultants:** Rambøll, Guy Nordenson and Associates, Ove Arup, L'Observatoire International, Vesa Honkonen Architects. **Gross area:** 2270 sq.m. **Cost ex VAT:** Approximately NOK 120 million. **Photos:** Iwan Baan and Steven Holl Architects

ENVIRONMENTAL INFORMATION: Estimated energy consumption: Not stated. **Average U value (W/sq.m.K):** Floor: 0.10, wall: 0.22, roof: 0.13, window: 1.1. **Energy sources:** Geothermal heat. Water-borne heating in all floors. **Ventilation:** Mechanical ventilation with heat recycler. **Materials:** Many local suppliers. Choice of non-toxic surface treatments. **Other measures:** The building has a small window area, and is well insulated.

04 FARM HOUSE TOTEN

JARMUND/VIGSNÆS ARKITEKTER

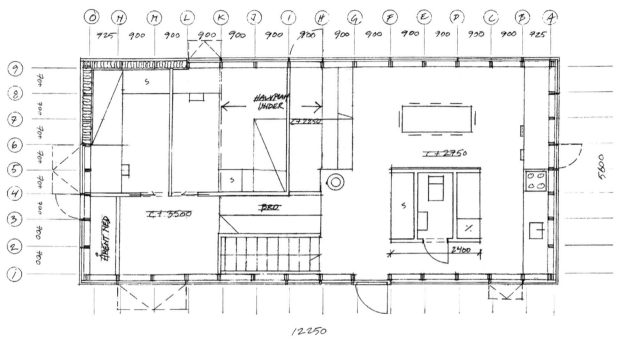

Ground/first floor plan.

A few simple moves turned a family house on a vacated farm into an innovative recycling project.

This is a small house for two historians and their children on a vacated farm that the couple inherited. The house is attractively situated at Toten in the county of Oppland with a view of Mjøsa, Norway's largest lake.

There were previously two buildings in the farmyard, a house and a barn. The house has been retained, but is uninsulated, and is now used only for occasional guests and for storage. The barn had to be demolished as there was rot in the load-bearing structure. However, the century-old panelling was still in good condition, and has been used as panelling and terraces for the new house. Some of the old planks had been cut to varying widths, and narrowed towards one end. These have been used to adjust the new horizontal panelling in relation to the gradient of the site and the angle of the roof.

The barn's spatial complexity, exposed structure and simple use of materials are clearly reflected in the new house. From the main entrance, the organisation of the house relates both to the view of the lake and to the terrace on the west side of the house. A series of stepped rooms provides a visual connection throughout the length of the house. The children's rooms are at the upper level and the parents' room is below. The main section opens towards the south to let in the low winter sun. The glass-clad conservatory functions as a heat store in winter and as a heat buffer in summer. The main structure is in timber with aluminium-clad windows. The basement floor is exposed concrete. The house is heated by water-borne underfloor heating and a wood stove.

Jarmund/Vigsnæs

PROJECT INFORMATION: Farm house, Toten. **Completed:** 2008. **Clients:** Ane Kristin Rogstad and Trond Nygård. **Architects:** Jarmund/Vigsnæs Arkitekter. **Team:** Einar Jarmund, Håkon Vigsnæs and Alessandra Kosberg with Nikolaj Zamecznik. **Gross area:** 165 sq.m. **Photos:** Nils Petter Dale.

ENVIRONMENTAL INFORMATION: Estimated energy consumption: 121 kWh/sq.m. GBA/year. **Land use:** 150 sq.m., 37.5 sq.m. per resident (4 persons). **Average U-value:** 0.334 W/sq.m.K.

05 ADMINISTRATION BUILDING FOR THE NORWEGIAN MINISTRY OF DEFENCE AND THE DEFENCE STAFF NORWAY. AKERSHUS FORTRESS, OSLO

JARMUND/VIGSNÆS ARKITEKTER
ØKAW ARKITEKTER

A long process of productive negotiations between architects, clients and conservation authorities allowed the Norwegian Ministry of Defence and the Defence Staff to stay in their historic location at Akershus fortress.

In connection with structural development of the Norwegian defence organisation, the Norwegian Parliament in 2002 decided to establish a new administration building for the Defence Staff and the Ministry of Defence at the Akershus Fortress. The project consists of a new building and a conversion of parts of the existing fortress, known as the Workshop Building.

Akershus Fortress has many historical layers. Some of these are the result of purposeful planning (e.g. Schirmer and von Hanno's plan dating from the 1800s), while others can be characterised as arbitrary, the consequences of refurbishments or unfinished plans.

In this respect, the Akershus Fortress site embodies a continual process of creation and transformation that we have sought to conserve and clarify.

The new programme demanded a transformation of the area. The overall aim of this transformation was to develop a modern office building with good internal communication between the various departments. The facility is intended to represent an open and accessible institution, while also satisfy-ing specific requirements regarding security, both in daily operations and in emergency situations. Regard for both antiquarian and organisational considerations required an exceptional degree of flexibility in the design. The solutions are based on the main principles of the urban perimeter block concept prepared in close cooperation with the conservation experts of the Directorate for Cultural Heritage and the Norwegian Defence Estates Agency.

The overall intention of the project has been to create a dialogue with the existing buildings, a dialogue that both refers to and discusses the past. A dark colour has therefore been chosen for the brickwork on the heavier parts of the new building, with reference to the use of brick particularly in the Arsenal and the Workshop Building. In order to continue this development of details, the windows have been placed in deep niches, with frame profiles concealed by the masonry. Sun shielding is integrated in the double glazing.

Jarmund/Vigsnæs and ØKAW Arkitekter

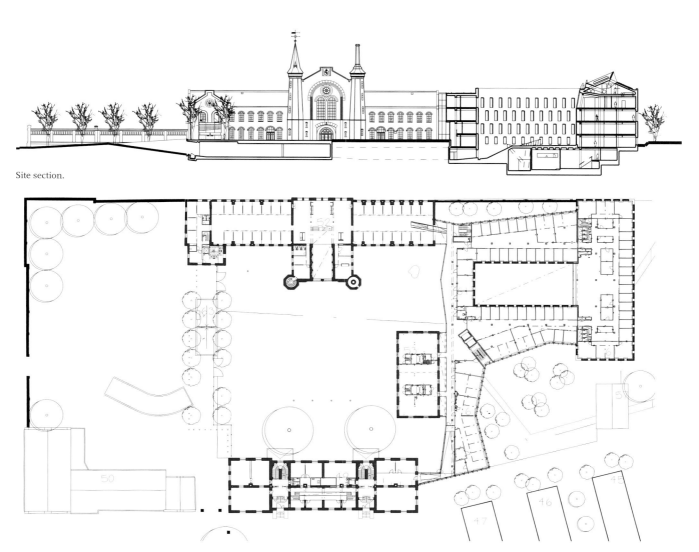

Site section.

Location plan.

PROJECT INFORMATION: Administration Building for the Norwegian Ministry of Defence and the Defence Staff Norway, Akershus Fortress. **Address:** Akershus Fortress, Oslo. **Client:** Norwegian Defence Estates Agency. **Built:** 2004–2006. **Architect for new building:** Jarmund/Vigsnæs Arkitekter. **Architect for conversion:** Økaw Arkitekter. **Interior architect:** Birgitte Appelong. **Landscape architect:** Grindaker. **Consultants:** Rambøll Norge. **Gross area:** 19 300 sq.m. **Cost:** Approx. NOK 560 million. **Photos:** Nils Petter Dale.

RESISTANCE AND PRECISION

INTERVIEW | **HÅKON VIGSNÆS, EINAR JARMUND AND ALESSANDRA KOSBERG
PARTNERS, JARMUND/VIGSNÆS ARKITEKTER**
BY INGERID HELSING ALMAAS

Jarmund / Vigsnæs AS describes itself as "a general store for architecture". All told, the office currently has about 40 large and small projects ongoing. And, although it has made its mark with large projects such as the Svalbard Science Centre in Longyearbyen (2005), the Oslo School of Architecture (2002) and the new administration building for the Defence Staff and the Ministry of Defence at the Akershus Fortress (2006), it is the many small projects that particularly characterise the activities of the office. Work on holiday cabins, family houses and alterations involves a continuous exploration of new architectural and technological solutions, which gradually turn familiar environments in new directions.

INGERID HELSING ALMAAS: You clearly enjoy the small projects?
HÅKON VIGSNÆS: We get close to people. These works are very important to the people involved, which makes us very enthusiastic.
ALESSANDRA KOSBERG: And it really builds up the pace of work at the office. Things are very intense for short periods while we are involved with the planning, and then the houses are built quite rapidly.

IHA: Is it possible to do things when designing family houses that are not so easy to achieve in larger buildings? With regard to both design and technology?
AK: There is very little repetition in a family house. You have the opportunity for considerable variation in individual programmes, and you can make them very different from other programmes.
HV: Another challenging aspect of building family houses is that this has become a sort of middle-class pheno-

"IF YOU CAN ONLY HAVE A LITTLE, YOU HAVE TO BASE YOUR WISHES ON SOME FORM OF INTELLIGENCE."

menon in Norway, and the clients often have limited funds. They often can't afford to do more than make alterations to an existing home. And this means that we have to really tune the solutions, to economise on space, site use etc. in order to make the most of what is available. Things often work out differently to what we think they will – more efficiently. And that resistance is a very valuable element. If you are designing a 1000 square metre holiday house, you don't meet the constraints that makes you smart.

EINAR JARMUND: We sometimes refer to this as a middle-class ethos: How to create paradise within a tight framework. And this is much more fun than the projects that have unlimited space and funding, where the freedom is only apparent.
HV: It is more difficult to question the ingrained conceptions of affluent people, because, if they see a picture in a magazine, they can afford to buy that particular dream.
EJ: It's a matter of being able to make priorities. If you can have anything you want, you're not able to make priorities. However, if you can only have a little, you have to base your wishes on some form of intelligence. And from this point of view, the big houses are at worst totally unintelligent.

Affordable material qualities

IHA: What about material qualities? Is there anything that is affordable to people with deep pockets that you feel like using?
HV: We are really more interested in using industrial products in other ways that result in a different quality, without necessarily going back to good craftsmanship, which is awfully expensive today. A house of ours, by the sea near

PHOTO: JARMUND/VIGSNÆS

Stavanger, is not an expensive house. It was built in sandwich concrete, which is regarded as almost impossible to use because it is so costly and difficult, but you can find that expertise at a reasonable price in this area, because of the oil industry.

IHA: What about experiments with form? Many of your small projects adopt forms that challenge people's conceptions regarding a family house or holiday cabin. Even among architects, there are probably many who take a sceptical view of sloping walls and sharp angles... What are you aiming for in terms of form?

HV: We try to free ourselves as far as possible in relation to each individual project. We force ourselves to think in terms of things not all being alike, of every challenge involving an element of originality, and this results in architecture that works well for the project concerned. At the same time, there are usually certain themes that we follow through two or three projects that we take a bit further. It's a matter of taking hold of some primary elements that we are looking for on the site, and aligning things in relation to them. That is very often what we are aiming for – these precise alignments. And that often twists things out of the orthogonal axes. Form is often driven by an interaction between an internal spatiality and external conditions. Considerations regarding landscape, views, access, gradients... And, if you disregard the rationalist arguments, there's nothing in the reality of architecture tying us to 90 degree angles. But in those cases where they are needed, where they are logical, we have no problems complying with the constraints imposed by right angles. Then they are an essential condition.

AK: I also think that the projects that are a bit more active designwise possibly escape the "house" concept: The box, the picture, the whole history of architecture with all previous references and relations to being a house. That is quite liberating...

Making the conditions clearer

IHA: The design language that you seem gradually to have developed breaks completely with what one normally expects, even in a world of attractive modern houses. At any rate, from a modernist point of view, it is the arbitrariness of the sloping angles that is the biggest objection against that type of architecture.

HV: We perceive our use of form as the opposite of arbitrary. That it is more an attempt to be precise in the situation. It is always a matter of making the conditions clearer.

EJ: Openness to several or many interpretations has become quite an important theme for us. We see that architecture only comes into being when someone looks at it.

HV: We want to open up for the users and viewers of the architecture.

EJ: And these viewers always have preconceptions of their own that we have no control over.

"OPENNESS TO SEVERAL OR MANY INTERPRETATIONS HAS BECOME QUITE AN IMPORTANT THEME FOR US."

IHA: But is it not more difficult to build something that has this greater precision designwise, as you define it?

AK: Not necessarily. For example, it makes it possible to conceal all structure. You can use very cheap materials inside the walls because they are clad, or on the walls, for example, because they are angled in such a way that they reflect the light differently, so the material is no longer the most important part of the story.

EJ: And it is not necessarily a goal that something should be easy to build, is it?

IHA: No, but the reference here is to the association between the constructive rationality of modernism and practice in today's building industry. For example, a carpenter would rather saw straight because sawing at an angle takes longer.

AK: But quality is dependent on skill in all parts of the process. And when you end up with a box lined with standard plasterboard that is completely uninteresting as a room, perhaps there is no place for quality anyway.

HV: It is a bit toothless to say, "Well, it's neofunctionalist, which is our legacy from the modernist approach", but then execute it just as latex-painted white plaster boxes.

AK: And then the new rooms just become exhibition rooms for Arne Jacobsen's red industrial products instead of having their own identity. And this is perhaps something we have tried to strive a little against.

The power of form

IHA: From the way you have now been arguing regarding the creation of architecture, it is actually suddenly very difficult to talk about form at all. But I want to try: In a discussion at the Venice Architecture Biennale in 2006, Zaha Hadid was challenged on the question of architectonic form. She was confronted with the view that her buildings could be seen as aimless preoccupation with form, a luxury in relation to construction and economy, an incomprehensible waste of resources rooted in a subjective artistic indulgence... She responded with a lengthy discussion culminating in a single utterance: "Don't knock form!" In other words, one should not dismiss the potential of architectonic form as if it were irrelevant, even when the form is challenged by all other rational aspects. We so easily attach importance to explaining everything we do, but architectonic form naturally has an aesthetic effect on people that, throughout many epochs of architectural history has been of central importance regardless of practical considerations.

HV: All epochs.

EJ: But even a shoebox is a form.

IHA: Yes, of course, but the issue is the will behind it, the purpose and intention: What is one trying to make?

EJ: When you consider Zaha Hadid's projects, you are of course completely bowled over by The Peak. If there is one significant competition project of hers, this is probably it. But it was precisely because it was such a correct response to the situation, to lead up to such a peak, and live a metropolitan life on the top with that view... It was a project associated with both expectations and references in relation to a very broad range, not only of forms, but also thoughts. While, if you look at her building at Ordrupgaard museum, outside Copenhagen in

Denmark, you wonder: Why does this look like this? There are very few points of contact with the programme or the location or what goes on there. What we are aiming for with all of our forms is to create such points of contact.

HV: And to combine a programme requirement on the one hand with an idea of light or some other situational quality on the other. So it's not at all certain that the straight line is the most straightforward way of doing things. And, in that respect, form has a broad range of functions in understanding a situation, and there is much more to it than just proving a theory about rational building.

References and ideals

IHA: Can you say something about your architectural ideals? One thing is the general references in the development of a form, but you surely also have things that you like? How do you relate to them and how do you use them?

EJ: We use them actively all the time. We find things at many levels... Alison and Peter Smithson, for example... The English fifties architecture, such matter-of-factness – that has been important and dear to us. Early Jim Stirling is also a forgotten high point. The Leicester University Engineering Building and the Florey Building in Oxford are absolutely fantastic... If there was ever someone who was able to take Le Corbusier's power of storytelling a step further, it was him.

HV: He was capable of handling pregnancy of meaning, the material that does more than just being in its apparently logical place in the hierarchy. He turned both constructive principles and use of materials upside-down.

EJ: In a very communicative way. To quote Peter Smithson, "Mies is great, but Corb communicates."

HV: Rudolf Schindler has been important for us. We're constantly returning to his...

EJ:...spatial sculptural treatment...

HV:...and ability to construe the location, his materiality, and strangeness. Unlike Frank Lloyd Wright, Schindler didn't just choose a theme and spin everything round that, he allowed himself a number of moves that made him seem a bit ec-

centric. And that is something that we are looking for too. Things must hold some surprises, be a bit strange. A bit ugly, perhaps.

AK: We too can work with the box. It's not that we have decided once and for all that we're not going to make boxes, but one has to be aware of the demands involved both when working within familiar frameworks and when working outside of them.

IHA: One also searches for natural forms in your work. But nothing of what you have said suggests that your use of form comes from associations with nature.

EJ: Well, that is one of our sources.

IHA: That a building should look like a boulder, for example.

EJ: It should, sometimes. That might sometimes be relevant.

"THINGS MUST HOLD SOME SURPRISES, BE A BIT STRANGE. A BIT UGLY, PERHAPS."

IHA: Metaphors, especially natural metaphors, are important to Norwegian architects. People understand them. In many projects, the persuasive power of the metaphor helps to protect the architectural concept through the process. For example, natural forms become an important argument for the project: If the building looks like an iceberg, it must be good.

EJ: But, to what extent does a metaphor actually tell a story? What we want is in many ways a narrative architecture, or to explore the narrative potential of the architecture. And an architectural story should not be clear and simple. It should have a broad range. This is possibly part of the experience we have gained from encountering so many old buildings. A great deal of our work has actually involved remodelling old things.

HV: Our buildings in Svalbard certainly look as if they have derived their form from nature. But those buildings are generated by a mental state in the landscape, by a need for shelter. How does one best tackle the climate conditions? How does one make one's building yield to nature so that it does not challenge

the forces unnecessarily, while at the same time creating the security that one needs, both physically and mentally? And then it is perhaps not so strange, in the light of these principles, that the same things happen as have happened to the landscape, where wind and weather have played their part, and there may be an interrelation between the aerodynamic requirements regarding the building and the geological erosion of the surrounding rocks. However, this is not brought about by imitating the natural form, it is derived from engaging with the location.

IHA: Like a kind of intuitive response?

EJ: A refinement of one's intuition.

HV: It is important to rework, refine the natural. In Norway, if you are to be honest and straightforward, you must definitely show the woodwork untreated, right? That is the "ultimate truth". But you can have a layer of piano lacquer between the woodwork and the world, that will preserve the wood, accentuate the fragility and say much more...

AK: We have talked about the fact that the solemn architect, the guardian of the truth, who after all characterised our student days, has been replaced by a different view of the world. You can investigate and experiment all you will, but you are not always completely aware of what themes you come into contact with.

HV: The architect was previously a law unto himself in a way. That is the opposite of what we want. Complexity is a method too; through open seminars, popular meetings and broad discussions, to find a symbiosis in the many parameters of a situation. That is were the originality lies.

Ingerid Helsing Almaas

...

Just a vague memory of walking from
one side of the city to the other,
alone, one night in January or February,
as in an old film from a polar landscape.

...

Tor Ulven

THE CHALLENGE OF **THE CITY**

Norway has a small population of only 4,8 million, spread over an area almost the size of Germany, and relatively few larger cities. These cities, however, face many of the same challenges as cities elsewhere in the world: rapid growth, economical changes and the need to stake out a new, sustainable direction for development. The search for an urban culture for the 21st century is on.

06 NEW HEADQUARTERS FOR GYLDENDAL PUBLISHERS OSLO

SVERRE FEHN

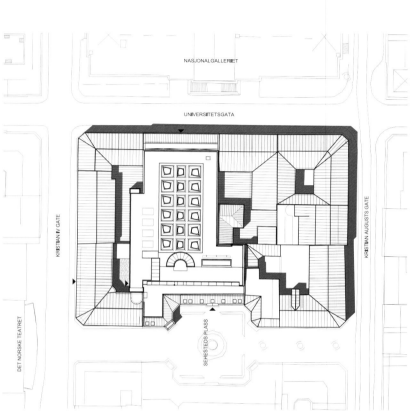

Location plan.

Reflecting the history of the publishing house as well as of the city, Sverre Fehn's rebuilding project is an urban storybox.

Gyldendal is Norway's largest publisher, but by 2005 its activities had expanded to the point where the publishing house occupied an entire block in the centre of Oslo. Over time the old-fashioned internal structure, with its maze of small rooms, had become impractical and difficult to work in. The architect commissioned to redesign the offices, with a view to keeping and restructuring the existing buildings. Thus the original facades were retained and a new building constructed within the old structure. A large central courtyard was created that contained the "Danish house", a copy of the original premises of the Danish mother company in Copenhagen. The main entrance is now the original gateway in Sehesteds plass, and the company's distinctive copper entrance door has been restored and moved from its previous position in Universitetsgaten to the new Sehesteds plass entrance.

The main plan is structured as an urban space, with exposed cylindrical columns, a tall ceiling and a succession of sculptural forms. The concrete wall at the entrance curves around the "theatre", a sunken amphitheatre with over a hundred seats, encircled by a balcony. The materials used throughout are light concrete, oak and dark textiles. In the ceiling are curved panels of oak veneer. Offices, meeting rooms, seminar rooms and writers' rooms are situated around the periphery of the luminous central space. This space is the heart of the building, and its generous dimensions are an open invitation to formal and informal meetings for exchanging experience, ideas and information, and to the organisation of cultural events and parties. The roof is formed of 18 pyramid-shaped concrete skylights of different sizes, set at different angles into pale concrete ribs. These spread the natural light entering the building, so that the play of light reflects the different seasons and time of day.

The layout allows for the flexibility needed by a busy publishing house in constant change.

Sverre Fehn

PROJECT INFORMATION: New Headquarters for Gyldendal Publishers, **Address:** Sehesteds Plass, Oslo. **Completed:** 2007. **Client:** Gyldendal. **Architect:** Sverre Fehn. **Team:** Sverre Fehn, Inge Hareide, Kristoffer Moe Bøksle, Halvor Kloster, Sjur Tveit, Henrik Hille, Baard Erlend Hoff, Marius Mowe, Martin Dietrichson. **3D and illustrations:** Young Fehn (Guy Fehn and Dennis Alekseev). **Interior architects:** ZINC, Hanne Margrethe Hjermann, Berit Olderheim and Cathrine Heyerdahl. **Landscape:** Sverre Fehn. **Gross area:** 9 000 sq.m.. **Cost ex. vat:** NOK 180 million. **Photos:** Ivan Brodey.

ENVIRONMENTAL INFORMATION: **Energy Sources:** District heating **Ventilation:** Mechanical with heat exchangers, locally controlled, **Materials:** Emphasis on long-term sustainable and environmentally friendly materials and flexibility in office layouts. Concrete structure with thermal mass inside insulation layer acts as energy buffer. Placement of windows reduces need for artificial lighting. Cladding is mostly re-used stone material.

"PEOPLE HAVE TO BE STRONG TO COPE WITH GOOD ARCHITECTURE"

INTERVIEW | **SVERRE FEHN**
BY INGERID HELSING ALMAAS

INGERID HELSING ALMAAS: The general impression abroad is that both traditional and contemporary Norwegian architecture is influenced by two things: our very close relationship with untouched nature, and our well developed skill at building in wood. Do you think there's anything in this?

SVERRE FEHN: The nature of Norway is nature untamed by cultivation. Here in Norway nature is the norm, whereas in many other places it is the cultivated land that people take for granted. In most parts of Europe almost every tree has been planted, while here, even in Oslo, you can build a villa, let's say a villa like Villa Schreiner, on pristine land. This aspect of nature in Norway is sensational. On the other hand, I don't think Norway has been especially innovative in this respect. When someone wants to build a house, they first cut down all the trees, then they sow a lawn, and plant a few plum trees [laughs], and then along the foundation wall they might put a row of tulips. It's as if you were to put a tree in a flowerpot in the middle of a wild landscape. It's quite moving, really, there's something fine about it [laughs]. But this form of culture isn't particularly inspired...

In Japan, for example, nature is enhanced, they cut off a couple of branches, and train and wire them, and make the tree smaller or larger and that sort of thing, you could almost say they torture nature...

IHA: But are Norwegians any kinder? Is this why they just plant a few plum trees?

SF: No, not at all, they're just naive. Or perhaps our nature is so harsh that we do everything we can to make it seem romantic and pretty. But you won't find anything especially inspired from an architectonic point of view. And then this

"IN NORWAY NATURE IS THE NORM, WHEREAS IN MANY OTHER PLACES IT IS THE CULTIVATED LAND."

passion for traditional log houses. All these farms and barns, they take up so much space, it's absurd to try to develop this trend any further today. This is also a form of romanticism that we haven't managed to do anything with – we really haven't managed to do much at all with the log.

IHA: So do Norwegians have a thoughtless approach to nature?

SF: Yes. Yes, you could say that.

Nature as metaphor

IHA: Architects have to make a real effort to get people to understand what they do. One of the easiest arguments to use is to associate the project with nature – contact with nature is something that almost everyone regards as positive, whether it's nature in terms of a lovely view, or a closer contact with the landscape and topography. In Norway it's easier to explain architecture with reference to nature, or by using natural metaphors, like calling the building an iceberg or a bird's nest. Isn't that a little too simple?

SF: Yes, but in Norway our relationship with nature is an active one, we escape into it as often as we can. You can't make contact with God unless you've been skiing! Every week! [Laughs.] So there is something in it. In some projects this relationship is a fundamental principle. You follow it to its logical conclusion and build something like the Glacier Museum, for example, which is a kind of altar to nature. You can go there and worship nature and find God in nature. But this idea hasn't been developed very far.

IHA: Does this kind of experience of

nature lead to anything? Some insight?

SF: Nature is basically cruel. Human nature is also fairly ruthless, and when it breaks out it can have quite violent results. We don't really understand very much about this aspect of nature. Our present culture is taking us further and further away from for instance perceiving the horse as an animal that pulls the plough or works as a war machine. The horse is being reduced to the level of aesthetics; it flies around a race track, and it's so beautiful you think you'll faint. But it's no longer anything more. Even though the horse is a fantastic thing that has shaped a lot of our technology. So in our culture we are moving further and further away from nature, and from nature as something that we use.

Architecture also follows these trends. But this means we can become like the Japanese, who have cultivated nature in relation to the home: sliding doors, a view you can look out on, the way you step down onto the ground, the stones placed before the threshold of a door, that kind of thing. Through their religious philosophy they've raised the use of nature to a philosophy, which has resulted in a very particular architecture. But if you try doing something like this in Norway, as I've tried to do in Villa Busk and Villa Schreiner for instance, it isn't really successful. In cases like this you work closely with nature and try to find a cultural expression that will achieve a dialogue with the trees already growing there. This is what I tried to do, but I didn't really manage it. But after all those houses are also in Europe, part of a tradition that includes Le Corbusier and his table structures, and his very different way of doing things... It was something like this I was thinking of when I created those houses. But in Norway we haven't done very much that reflects the relationship between nature and architecture.

IHA: Why is this? Is it because over the last two generations people in Norway have been so prosperous that it hasn't been necessary for most people to think very hard about anything, or because before that we lived under such demanding conditions that we weren't able to think about anything other than our basic needs? After all, Norway was one of the poorest countries in Europe before the success story of Norwegian oil began in 1970?

SF: No, we don't have a philosophy on which to base our ideas. We have a concept of God, but that's still rooted in Palestine and the country of the Jews, which is natural I suppose... But when we try to imagine that God is here, with us, we turn to nature to find out what constitutes the sacred and the holy... But then, Norwegians' worship of nature consists merely of going as fast as you can as far as you can – it's just an achievement. You climb to the top of a mountain and look at the spectacular view and so on, but this form of belief is really quite a simple one.

"NORWEGIANS' WORSHIP OF NATURE CONSISTS MERELY OF GOING AS FAST AS YOU CAN AS FAR AS YOU CAN."

IHA: But nature isn't anything in itself. When you stand on a mountaintop and look at the view and say "Isn't this a marvellous view?", it's not nature that's marvellous, nature just is. You are the one who feels marvellous on your mountaintop.

SF: Yes, that's right.

Norwegian cities

IHA: But what about our cities?

SF: If we do have any cities. Well, the cities are there, there are urban places in Norway, but only just. The cities are very small.

Because people live so close to each other, cities need a love of other people. You have to like shoes, your hat and coat, you must become a distinctive figure in a place. You have to love looking at another individual – the clothes they're dressed in, what they're carrying, what mask they're wearing. This is what makes a city. I think this actually has to do with laziness – because people think cities are productive, but they don't actually produce anything. The production of a city serves idleness: chairs, jewels, a beautiful dress, beds and tables

are conceived and produced in cities. Everywhere in a city, even on the street, you'll find places to sit. When a culture has developed up to a certain point, people have time, they have time to sit, and to think. This is the nature of the city, sitting and thinking and waiting – for a war, for the boat to leave, working out how to earn money.

As soon as you're in the countryside, you're immediately involved in production – the hay has to be brought in, the cow has to be milked and it's a hell of a life [laughs]. You can't turn round without having something to do. But the city is a kind of container; the most natural thing in a city is the chemist's, where the poisons are locked up...

IHA: Well, in the countryside they have time off as well...

SF: No, they bloody well haven't.

IHA: ... for weaving rugs and decorating their things...

SF: No, they sneak some time in for those activities during the winter [laughs]. I remember being interested in the fishermen on the Spanish coast, that was before all the hotels were built there. I was filming the fishermen's houses down by the water. But although their boats are drawn up on the beach, the first thing they build is a wall, and then a house behind it, and then they can't see the sea from inside the house. It's not until they open the door that they come in contact with production, the beauty of nature, the fish and grey skies and hard work. And then they go into their little walled-in houses, all clustered together.

IHA: Perhaps to get away from the sea ?

SF: Yes, to avoid looking at their factory. But this leads to very beautiful dwellings, very organised and well thought out... But if one perceives the city as a function of the waiting I mentioned above, the situation changes completely. In a city, thieves give rise to law courts, and morality gives rise to the church and the monastery, and this is quite different from thinking in terms of production.

Protective pavilion covering new excavations. Hedmark Museum, Hamar 2005.
PHOTO: HELENE BINET

Villa Schreiner, Oslo 1963.
PHOTO: AFTENPOSTEN

Architecture and democracy

IHA: What's it like being an architect in a democracy? Building projects are large scale operations and involve a lot of money and a lot of people. As an architect, you have to make decisions on behalf of others, and sometimes your decisions have to be altered to fit in with other considerations and interests?

SF: Yes, but in urban architecture you must always have an initial idea, a proposal. Today proposals have become so democratised that it's no longer a real proposal. The user or the developer is actually the one to submit a proposal, but they don't go through the government bureaucracy, they go straight to let's say the city council, and it's the political parties represented in the council who then make the decision... It's no longer a question of beauty or size or anything like that, it's a question of whether the developer has the right contacts. This leads to a city based on commerce, which is what Oslo is becoming. There's no brake that can be applied to such a process. But you don't actually need a brake, you need a positive proposal. If you had an architectural competition, or a City Architect or planner with a vision...

IHA: Perhaps this also has something to do with resistance, like in our discussion about nature? These forces also need some resistance to develop?

SF: Yes, you have to be able to put a brake on the process... Because the people on the city council aren't experts, poor things! But I've noticed that if a client is presented with a really interesting project, they usually go along with it. But you must always be in a position to make a proposal.

IHA: Would you say that the more complex or diffuse the commission is, the more important it is to find one's own approach? In order to present this initiating proposal?

SF: Yes, of course. And the weaker the client, the more you have to contribute, the two have to balance each other. And yet, if you provide a weak man with a solution, he'll actually be afraid of it, because it shows up his weakness. I think people have to be very strong to cope with good architecture.

IHA: If you're going to persuade others to adopt your proposal, you need a strong argument. But must one have the gift of persuasion in order to be an architect? In order to produce a good design?

SF: No, not at all – as Matisse once said, if you want to be a painter, cut out your tongue. But you have to be able to persuade people and so on ...

IHA: But in this case wouldn't it be tempting to go with the design that is easiest to explain? That is the easiest to justify?

SF: Yes, but you're anyway always trying to find the simplest solution. There are a lot of factors you have to take into account, but a simple solution often provides answers to several different questions. But you can't just begin building, you have to reach an architectonic expression before you start. The drawing is vital. To be a good architect actually requires great humility. You have to make the most of the very small amount of knowledge you possess. Many young people today don't have the patience. In my time we had to make maximum use of what little we had. In my case what remained was a tiny little villa – this sort of thing is mainly what I've been doing. And this kind of humility, or patience, is basically missing in our society today.

Ingerid Helsing Almaas

This interview took place in Fehn's office in Oslo, Thursday 18th September 1997.

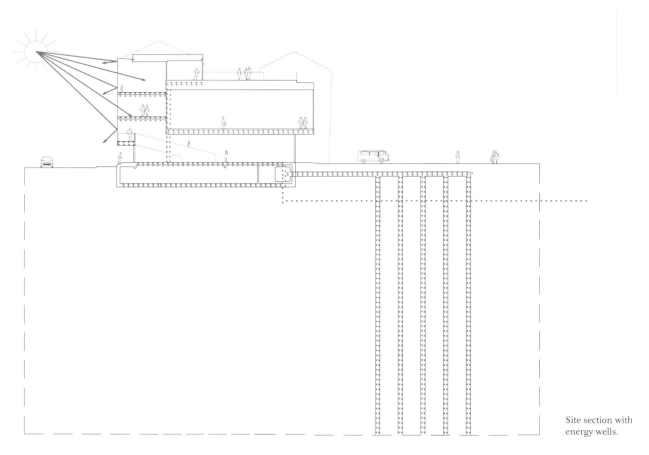

Site section with
energy wells.

Glass doesn't have to be an environmental liability. In a conference centre in the middle of Oslo, large glass façades are combined with an ambitious low energy concept.

Lærernes Hus (Teachers' House), the new conference centre of the Union of Education Norway, lies in the centre of Oslo, and is organised on four floors: lobby on the first floor, conference hall on the second floor and café and roof terrace on the third floor. The cloakroom, toilets and technical rooms are located in the basement. The rear building of an existing townhouse contains, among other things, a fire escape, storeroom and kitchen. The main focus of the project has been to create a building that is both energy- and environmentally friendly. This has resulted in a low-energy building with energy consumption estimated at only 80 kWh/sq.m. per year, achieved by a combination of the choice of materials and efficient energy solutions: ten energy wells, a heat pump and cast-in water pipes in floor decks and in the main staircase. The additional cost of the energy wells and the heat pump has a payback period of three to five years. In addition to this, LED lighting has been used, which has a long lifetime and low energy consumption. The decoration of the main façade functions as sun screen and further improves the energy efficiency.

The main approach has been to create an interplay between a large conference hall and integrated art in the façade, symbolising the central role of the client organisation in education and training. The building is adapted to the heights and the roof lines of the neighbouring buildings on both sides. The building has light from both sides on all floors, and the café is set back to secure the daylight and openness towards the surrounding courtyards. A gently rising main staircase begins in the lobby and runs parallel to the glass façade. The risers are low and the steps deep to encourage slow movement. There are two coffee bars on the landings, inviting people to use the staircase as a vertical lobby.

The main materials are light in-situ concrete combined with glass façades facing the conference hall, the street and the rear courtyard. The street façade is supported by continuous vertical glass fins. Integrated artwork, developed in close cooperation with the artists, gives the building a unique and personal expression.

Element Arkitekter

ENVIRONMENTAL INFORMATION: Estimated energy consumption: Less than 80 kWh/sq.m. per year (class A). **Average U-value (W/m2K):** Main glass façade 1.3 (glass 1.1); other glass façades 1.6–1.9; outer wall 0.21; roof 1.1–1.2; ground floor 0.16. **Energy solution:** The building draws energy for heating from ten energy wells (150 to 200 metres deep), drilled in the back-yard. During the summer, the building is cooled by the cold water drawn up from the energy wells. The building is mainly heated by means of underfloor heating in addition to the effect of sunlight through the glass façades. Apart from this, the main source of energy is electricity, which is used for lighting, kitchen, pumps, ventilation and the heat pump. **Ventilation:** Needs-controlled balanced mechanical ventilation. **Use of materials:** The use of sealed concrete surfaces and oiled wooden flooring results in low evaporation and pollution. The same applies to glass and panels. **Universal design:** Open rooms and the central location of the elevator facilitate orientation in the building. In order to ensure access for wheelchair users, an elevator stop has been installed at street level and a wheelchair elevator has been installed in the existing premises.

PROJECT INFORMATION: Teachers' House, Union of Education Norway Conference Centre. Address: Osterhaus Gate 4, Oslo. **Completed:** 2009. **Client:** Union of Education Norway. **Architect:** Element Arkitekter. **Team:** Cathrine Vigander, Vidar Knutsen, Hallvard Huse, Alexander Wærsten, Ines Almeida. Elisabeth Bjørge, interior architect. **Landscape architect:** Trifolia Landskapsarkitekter. **Artist, facade decoration:** Jorunn Sannes. **Consultant:** Jan Petter Dybdal. **Gross area:** 1794 sq.m. **Cost ex VAT:** approx. NOK 38 million (building cost excl. exterior and energy wells). **Photos:** Element Arkitekter

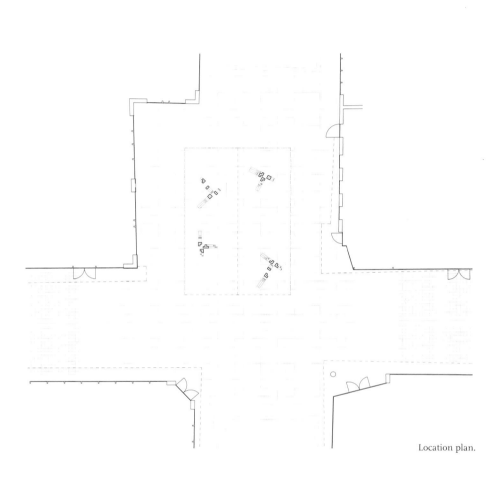

Location plan.

An open public space with a suspended roof in the middle of Sandnes has given the old quarter of the town a new focus and made the city centre more attractive.

Development of the sea front in Sandnes in recent years has meant that the commercial harbour and industry has been displaced by housing, shopping centres, hotels, a civic centre and a college. Langgata is a street in the old quarter of the town, a busy pedestrian area with market, shops, cafés and nightlife. However, the old quarter is cut off from the sea by the railway, a challenge for which Sandnes Town Council has wanted to find a solution. As part of the "Norwegian Wood" project, it was decided that a roof would be erected over the central square in Langgata, to add an attraction to the old quarter and meet the increasing competition from the harbour area.

The semitransparent roof structure, with its iconographic barn shape, is supported by clustered oak columns. The columns spread out to distribute the weight of the roof and stabilize the structure. Benches and service conduits have been integrated into the columns. It was originally proposed that the roof structure should be a self-supporting double shell of composite materials, epoxy or polyester, but this was not permitted since it involved use of solvents. Finally, the natural choice was found to be wood and glass, in the form of a three-dimensional latticework, constructed of narrow wooden staves. The columns are constructed of 150 x 150 mm solid oak. The columns can remain untreated, and the hardness of the oak will help to withstand mechanical wear and tear in an exposed urban environment. The wooden structure is covered by a weatherproof skin of glass plates, overlapped to enable the glass to be mounted directly on the wooden framework without the use of steel profiles or sealants.

AWP/Atelier Oslo

PROJECT INFORMATION: The Lantern – Covered square in Sandnes.
Address: Langgata, Sandnes. **Completed:** 2008. **Client:** Sandnes local author-
ity. **Architects:** AWP and Atelier Oslo. **Team:** AWP: Matthias Armengaud,
Alessandra Cianchetta, Sebastien Demont, Aurelien Masurel, Arnaud
Hirschauer, Marc Armengaud, Atelier Oslo: Jonas Norsted, Marius Mowe,
Siri Hopperstad, Anette Johansen, Bosheng Gan, Thomas Liu, Nils Ole Bae
Brandtzæg. **Photos:** Emilie Ashley and Thomas Liu

ENVIRONMENTAL INFORMATION: Materials: Main structure made
from solid, untreated oak, protected by glass panels. Prefabricated pole structure with column bundles in solid oak. Prefabricated roof structure in pine.

09 | OSLO OPERA HOUSE OSLO
SNØHETTA

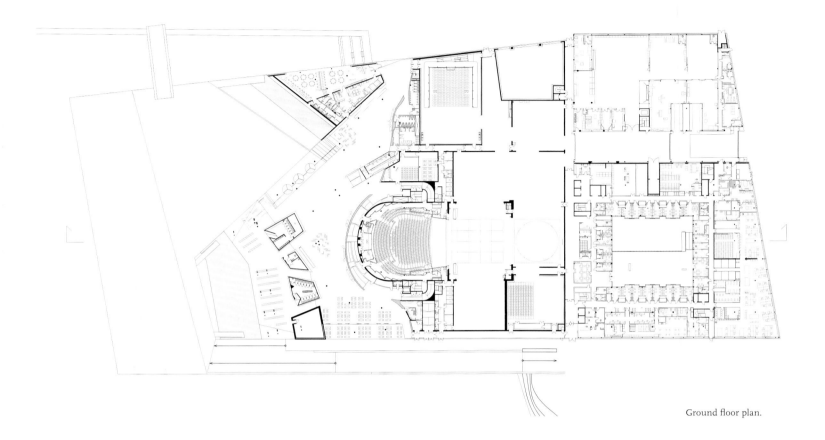

Ground floor plan.

The new Opera House has created a new urban space in the heart of a large transformation area in the centre of Oslo. As well as the performance spaces, the foyers and the fully accessible roofscape has been embraced by the citizens.

The Bjørvika pier forms one side of Oslo's inner harbour basin, and has for centuries been one of Oslo's points of contact with the world. However, with the decline in harbour activity, the site became underused and was in a state of decay. The Opera House was conceived as a lever for upgrading this part of the city and help transform it into a mixed use development area.

Programme and general organisation
The building links the city with the fjord, and the hills to the east with the historical centre of the city to the west. It marks the contrast between the solid earth here and the fluid water there, and is at the same time a meeting point between land and sea, Norway and the world, art and everyday life - the point where the public meets the artist.

The design for the Opera House was the winning entry in the international architectural competition in 2000. The building programme was complex, and naturally changes were made during the process, but the basic concept proposed in the competition entry has been retained.

The building concept consists of three parts: the Wave Wall, the Factory and the Carpet. The Wave Wall separates the public areas from the stage, and the immense four-storey-high oak wall symbolises the threshold that the public must cross in order to meet the arts of opera and dance. The Factory is the production area, while the Carpet is the 18 000 sq.m. marble roofscape that gives the building its monumental quality.

The interior of the building is divided into two by a north–south corridor called the Opera Street, which serves as the main communication artery for the staff: almost 600 people

representing 50 different occupations. The Factory is situated on the east side of the Opera Street, and consists of almost 1000 rooms of varying sizes and different functions.

On the west side of the Opera Street lie the public areas and the stages. These have a freer form and in some cases very high ceilings. A marble-clad plaza leads the public to the main entrance and the foyer, which has a vast glazed south-facing wall that provides a panoramic view over the Oslo Fjord. The building can accommodate up to 2000 people on a performance night, approximately 1400 in the main auditorium, 400 in Stage 2 and 150 in Rehearsal Room 1.

The main auditorium

The main auditorium is a classic horseshoe theatre built for opera and ballet, with 1370 seats.

The orchestra pit is highly flexible and the height and area can be adjusted to three separate sizes. On either side of the stage are mobile towers that allow the width of the proscenium to be adapted to ballet or opera. Reverberation time is fine-tuned by drapes along the rear walls. The architectonic intention – a modern auditorium for the appreciation of traditional, unamplified musical expressions – was developed to meet the visual intimacy and acoustic excellence required by the building programme. In older opera halls, acoustic attenuation was often achieved by the use of richly decorated sculptural elements on walls, ceilings and balconies, but in the present case a modern architectonic language has been used. The double curvature of the balcony fronts and the oval ceiling ring consist of pre-fabricated oak elements made of solid pieces glued together, treated with ammonia and then oiled and polished.

Art and materials

Snøhetta believes in close collaboration with the artists during all building projects. Right from the competition phase the architect's intention was to involve the artists in the design of both the large marble-clad roofscape and the aluminium-clad facades. At an early stage of the competition three main materials were specified: white stone for the Carpet, timber for the Wave Wall, and metal for the Factory, giving it an industrial look. The Italian marble La Facciata was chosen for the Carpet and oak for the Wave Wall and the floor, walls, balcony fronts, reflectors and ceilings. The metal panels were punched with convex spherical segments and concave conical forms; the pattern was developed by the artists on the basis of traditional weaving techniques.

Snøhetta

PROJECT INFORMATION:
Oslo Opera House, **Address:** Kirsten Flagstads plass 1, Oslo. **Completion:** 2007, opening 12th April 2008. **Client:** Statsbygg – Public Construction and Property Management. **Commissioning ministry:** Ministry of Culture and Church Affairs. **End user:** The Norwegian National Opera & Ballet. **Architect:** Snøhetta AS. **Interior architect:** Snøhetta. **Landscape architect:** Snøhetta.
Architectural competition phase:
Project architects: Craig Dykers, Tarald Lundevall, Kjetil Trædal Thorsen. **Architects:** Martin Dietrichson, Ibrahim El Hayawan, Harriet Rikheim, Marianne Sætre, Chandani Ratnawira. **Landscape architects:** Ragnhild Momrak. **Artistic advisors:** Inger Buresund, Axel Hellstenius, Henrik Hellstenius, Peder Istad, Jorunn Sannes. **Theatre consultants:** Theatre Projects Consultants.
Planning and building phase:
Project manager: Tarald Lundevall. **Assistant management:** Sigrun Aunan, Craig Dykers, Simon Ewings. **Design leader:** Kjetil Trædal Thorsen. **Group leaders architects:** Rune Grasdal, Elaine Molinar, Tom Holtmann. **Team architects:** Ibrahim El Hayawan, Frank Kristiansen, Camilla Moneta, Frank

Nodland, Harriet Rikheim, Margit Tidemann Ruud, Marianne Sætre, Ingebjørg Skaare, Anne-Cecilie Haug, Tine Hegli, Jette Hopp, Zenul Khan, Cecilia Landmark, Aase Kari Mortensen, Andreas Nygaard, Michael Pedersen, Knut Tronstad, Tae Young Yoon. **Group leader landscape:** Kari Stensrød. **Team landscape architects:** Ragnhild Momrak, Andreas Nypan.
Group leaders interiors: Øystein Tveter, Bjørg Aabø. **Team interior architects:** Christina Sletner.
Artists: Integrated art on the stone clad surfaces: Kristian Blystad, Kalle Grude, Jorunn Sannes. Integrated art on the metal clad facades: Astrid Løvaas, Kirsten Wagle. Cladding on foyer volumes: Olafur Eliasson. Stage curtain: Pae White.
Consultant engineers: Reinertsen Engineering (structure), NGI (geological engineering), Ingeniør Per Rasmussen (electrical), Erichsen & Horgen (H&V), Brekke Strand Akustikk, Arup Acoustic (acoustics), Theatre Project Consultants (theatre planning and stage technical services), Rambøll Sverige (sub stage technical services).
Gross area: 38 500 sq.m., Public areas: 11 200 sq.m., Stage areas: 8 300 sq.m., Rehearsal spaces, workshops, administration: 19 100 sq.m., Footprint:

15 590 sq.m., Length, incl. entrance plaza: 242 m, Width: 110 m. Gross height stage: 54 m, sub stage, depth below sea level: 16 m. No. of seats main theatre: 1 360, no. of seats stage 2: 400. **Project cost, adjusted to 2008 levels:** 4,023 billion NOK (€ 500 million)
Photos: Hélène Binet, Ivan Brodey, Statsbygg, Kim Nygård

ENVIRONMENTAL INFORMATION:
Calculated energy use per year: 215 kWH/kvm.
Energy sources: District heating, solar panels.
Ventilation: Mechanical ventilation with high level of heat recovery and user control.
Material use: Extended use of stone and wood, low emission materials.
Other: Passive measures to avoid draughts, sunscreening to avoid the need for cooling, use of solar panels as sunscreening; movement detector lighting controls.

NICHOLAS H. MØLLERHAUG

Brown snake in a white casket

White casket
by the sea.

Casket of salt.
Casket of sugar.
Casket of bone.

The brown snake
in the white casket.
Glides in oil, makes not a sound.

A casket of bone, salt
and sugar
by the water.

***

Arias.
High.
Low.
In the snake acoustics.
Venom gathered
in a sun.

The sun
hangs under the ceiling above us.
Clean light free from venom.

Undress.
Bathe in the sun as you sing.
The sun gives light to the whole
stage and the whole hall.

The tenor breaks
the bread asunder
The bass throws the bread to the people.
Soprano looking to the snake.
Alto looking to the snake.

The snake eats no bread.

***

White casket
by the sea.

A brown snake
in the white casket.

***

Now shut your mouth.
You will eat, and no singing.

***

White casket
by the sea.

A brown snake
in the white casket.

***

After a night
at the opera
the mind is
glossed with oil.

Concentrated oil
quiet.

After a night
at the opera
the walls
are
glossed with oil.

Oil where the snake glides without
sound.

Oil in the
dark churches:

Oil in Urnes

Oil in Heddal

Oil in Ulvik

Oil in these walls.

Oil in Uvdal

Oil in Røldal

Oil in Hopperstad

Oil in Rødven

Oil in these walls.

Oil in Kaupanger

Oil in Stange

Oil in Reinli

Oil in Nore

Oil in these walls.

Oil in Bø

Oil in Mære

Oil in these walls.

Oil in the dark churches

Oil in these walls.

Nicholas H. Møllerhaug

Commissioned by Arkitektur N on the occasion of the
opening of the Oslo Opera House, April 2008. English translation
by Ingerid Helsing Almaas

...

If this is not democratic enough,

if the city is as large as this square

if the city is no larger

then you are not large enough for this society

...

Tone Hødnebø

THE CHALLENGE OF **COMMUNITY**

The Scandinavian welfare state is a well-known model. But how are the resources managed by the state and local authorities, and how are the needs, interests and priorities of the community expressed in architecture? Architecture has the capacity to bring people together, in familiar and unfamiliar ways.

10 | NANSEN PARK
FORNEBU, BÆRUM
BJØRBEKK & LINDHEIM LANDSKAPSARKITEKTER

The site of the former main airport at Fornebu has been converted from a busy, noisy, polluted strip to a sculptural environment and recreation park.

The new Nansen Park was opened in September 2008. The park is part of an extensive transformation of Fornebu, Norway's former main airport just outside Oslo. Closure of the airport in 1998 freed up an enormous area of land, enabling one of the largest clearance and redevelopment projects in the country. An entirely new community is to be developed, complete with dwellings, services and infrastructure, and in the middle of it a large unifying recreation area, the Nansen Park.

The area is situated on a peninsula with wide open spaces surrounded by the sea and by Oslo's hilly landscape. Guiding principles for the design of the park have been the experience of tranquillity, beautiful views and harmonious forms, coupled with opportunities for physical recreation. The landscape architects have attempted to restore the soft, organic forms of the original landscape in dynamic interaction with the taut, straight lines of the former airport.

The old airport control tower and the former terminal building to the north constitute "Tower Square", which forms the entry point to the park. From here, a watercourse runs from north to south throughout the length of the park, receiving the surface water from adjacent housing areas and roads. Open green channels and swales have been established to carry the water down to a central lake, where it is purified by biological sand filters, mechanical strainers and pumps.

Other collection points are the "Festival Plaza" and the "Strip", with clear reference to the former runway. The Strip has been formed by layering various materials characteristic of Fornebu's geology. Broad granite steps lead down to the

lake, which is flanked by a broad wooden deck, a strip of river pebbles and an area of polished concrete embedded with green runway lights. The Festival Plaza has a floor of large, bevelled granite flagstones. To the south, the floor slopes evenly down into the lake.

A large amphitheatre is available for performances of various kinds, or just as a quiet place to sit. There are plans for a café adjacent to the Festival Plaza.

Seven arms of the park, with widths varying from 30 to 100 metres, reach out in all directions, enabling people to move around all over Fornebu. Various recreational activities have been located in these arms, such as sand volleyball courts, adventure playground, a large climbing net and wooden sitting, running and rolling elements. The various parts of the Nansen Park are connected by a network of walkways/cycleways as well as narrow gravelled paths.

A strong ecological profile forms the foundation for the whole transformational process. Polluted grounds have been cleaned. Asphalt and concrete have been retrieved and reused. New soil for cultivation has been made from masses from the site, with the addition of composted sewer sludge. Large volumes of earth and rock have been moved within the Fornebu area in order to transform the flat airport area into a landscape with different spatial qualities. Importance has been attached to using eco-labelled materials. Future maintenance is also to be carried out in accordance with ecological principles.

Bjørbekk & Lindheim

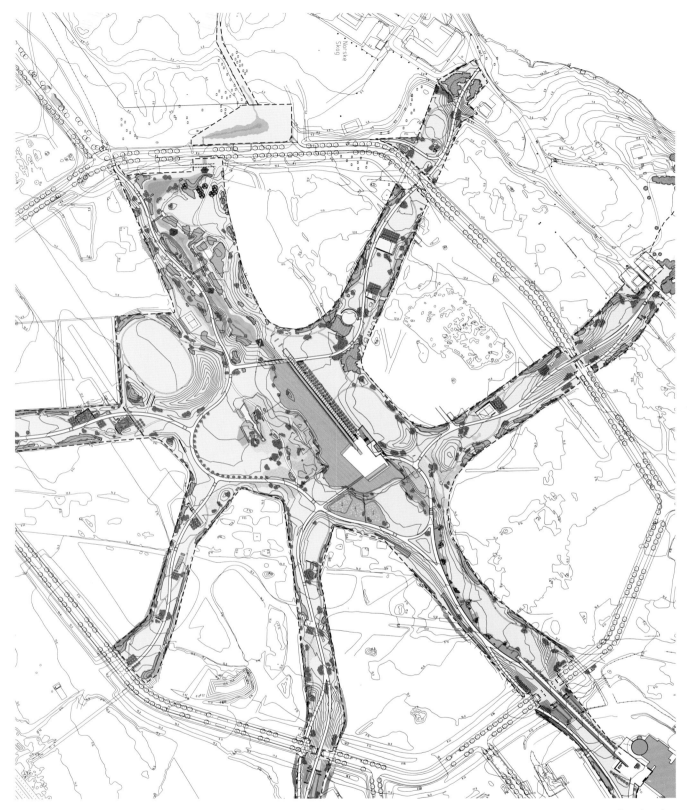

Location plan.

PROJECT INFORMATION: Nansen Park. **Address:** Fornebu, Bærum.
Client: Statsbygg – Public Construction and Property Management and Oslo
Municipality. **Completed:** 2008. **Area:** 20 hectares. **Cost:** NOK 120 million.
Landscape architect: Bjørbekk & Lindheim. **Team:** Tone Lindheim (project
manager), Svein Erik Bergem, Simen Gylseth, Knut H. Wiik, Line Løvstad
Nordbye, Håvard Strøm, Rune Vik and Christer Ohlsson. **Consultants:**
Norconsult. **Artistic consultant for water:** Atelier Dreiseitl. **Photos:** Bjørbekk &
Lindheim and Andreas Øverland.

NARUD-STOKKE-WIIG

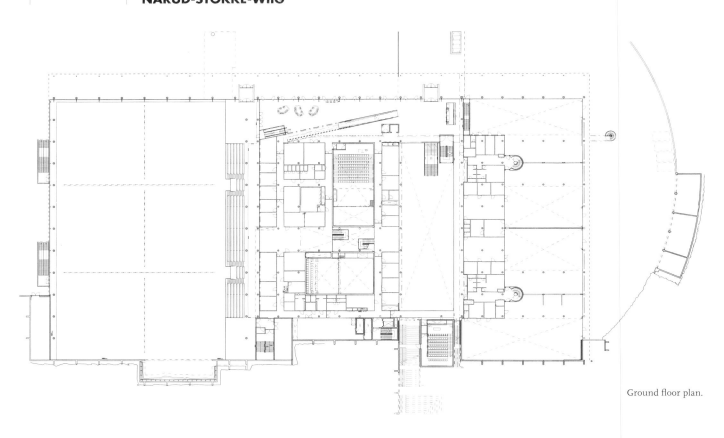

Ground floor plan.

Bjørnholt School unites architecture with politics and pedagogy. Built for over 1000 students, it is a large school with social ambitions.

Bjørnholt School in the south of Oslo has been designed with new pedagogical concepts in mind. This requires rooms to be dimensioned differently to a traditional upper secondary school. Learning takes place in open common areas shared by different subjects, surrounded by group rooms of various sizes, laboratories and work rooms. This results in effective use of space, but entails a more complex and demanding planning process. The volumes must be large, open and transparent, and there are special requirements regarding fire safety and escape routes, noise and acoustics and, not least, ventilation, heating, cooling and lighting. Importance has been attached to the need for mingle areas, seating units and open circulation areas adapted to various sizes of student groups. The basic concept of the school requires co-use of functions by the different areas of study, and the fundamental visions carry political goals associated with integration and learning in a neighbourhood with a large multicultural population. Bjørnholt has courses for the International Baccalaureate as well as courses in media, music, dance and drama and building and construction. This results in a lively and varied environment.

The school and the indoor sports arena, is built as a self-contained building complex, where the unifying element is the roof. The school building itself is divided into two parts, with a semi-glass-covered area between them. This area is occupied by the library, which is also open to the local population. The various academic departments are placed around communal areas and a canteen. Each department has its own group rooms and seminar rooms and workshops, staff rooms and course administration. Auditoriums, shared group rooms, learning and self-study areas are located in the centre of the building. The vocational courses have well-equipped workshops with access for vehicles and their own laboratories, an IT department and a department for special needs education. On the opposite side is the Department for Music, Dance and Drama, with "black boxes" on two floors. There is also an adapted education department for autistic pupils and other pupils with special needs. This has a separate entrance and a protected outdoor area.

The materials have a rough character with a lot of visible in-situ concrete combined with steel and glass. Bold colours and forms flirt with an otherwise cool expression.

Narud-Stokke-Wiig

PROJECT INFORMATION: Bjørnholt Upper Secondary School. **Address:** Slimeveien, Oslo. **Completed:** 2007. **Client:** Undervisningsbygg/Oslo Municipality. **Architect:** Narud-Stokke-Wiig. **Team:** Jørn Narud, Aylin Jørgensen-Dahl, Kjell Dybedal, Håvard Fagernes, Tai Grung, Live Hjelde, Randi Holmen, Emil Kristansen, Ellen Sjong, Jan-Ellef Søyland, Kaja Tiltnes, Erlend Torkildsen, Sjur Tveit, Stefan Krauel, Haukur Morthens. **Fittings and equipment:** Mirjana Grahovac. **Landscape architect:** Multiconsult/Link Landskap. **Gross area:** 27200 sq.m. incl. sports arena. **Cost ex VAT:** NOK 680 million incl. outdoor work, fittings, equipment. **Photos:** Jiri Havran.

ENVIRONMENTAL INFORMATION: Estimated energy consumption: School: 215 kWh/sq.m. per year, Multi-purpose hall: 234 kWh/sq.m. per year. **Weighted average:** 219 kWh/sq.m. per year. **Gross area per student:** 19.1 sq.m. Incl. indoor sports arena, per student: 24.7 sq.m. **Average U value:** Dense surfaces: 0.172 W/sq.m.K, glass surfaces: 1.35 W/sq.m.K. **Energy sources:** District heating. **Ventilation:** Mechanical ventilation. Forced draft ventilation is used in all rooms with high ceilings. **Use of materials:** All interior surface materials have low emissions. Anti-radon measures have been carried out in the school buildings.

12 ARENA BEKKESTUA BÆRUM

B+R / BRØGGER & REINE ARKITEKTUR

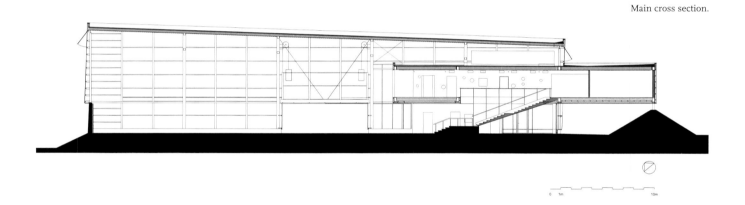

Main cross section.

A progressive programme, developed with extensive user involvement, has given a facility accommodating innovation and physical activities for young people.

Arena Bekkestua at Nadderud Sports Park just outside Oslo is a multi-use facility for young people. It has an activity area of approximately 1000 sq.m. indoors, and approximately 3000 sq.m. outdoors. Activities accommodated by the facility include skateboarding, BMX, inline, new circus, dance, concerts and fashion shows. Arena is intended to meet the activity needs of a constantly changing youth culture. While the facility is designed for current activities, it must be rapidly adaptable to new ones. With this point of departure, the architects have created flexible areas with potential for different uses.

By varying the size and degree of finish of the areas, the building satisfies a wide variety of needs. This is most clearly manifest in the juxtaposition of the two main volumes of the building: a hall designed for rough activities and an inserted section with a higher degree of finish. Large doorways in the long sides of the hall connect outdoor and indoor areas. Areas of glass and translucent plastic also provide different forms of exposure. The building has a daily average of about 300 visitors in addition to events for up to 1200 people.

Youth representatives took part in the programming and planning of the facility. Owing to their diversity and their ability to enthusiastically engage and promote participation, the activities of the young cultural practitioners provide a central arena for the formation of identity, dissemination of knowledge and general socialising.

b+r / Brøgger & Reine

PROJECT INFORMATION: Arena Bekkestua. **Address:** Gamle Ringeriks-vei 55, Nadderud Idrettspark, Bærum. **Completed:** 2006. **Client:** Bærum local authority. **Architect:** b+r / Brøgger & Reine arkitektur. **Team:** Lasse Brøgger, Anne-Stine Reine, Hans Kristian Moen. **Gross area:** 1 200 sq.m. **Photos:** Simon Skreddernes, b+ r.

ENVIRONMENTAL INFORMATION: Estimated energy consumption: 170 kWh/sq.m./year. The hall has been planned as a semi-climatised zone, heated to 8 degrees C. The remainder of the building has a normal comfort temperature of 20 degrees C. **U-values:** The hall has walls of polycarbonate channel boards with a U-value of 1.20 W/sq.m.K. Elsewhere: walls: 0.22 W/sq.m.K, ceiling: 0.15 W/sq.m.K, doors/windows: 1.60 W/sq.m.K. **Energy sources:** Water-borne radiator heating and air recirculation heaters. The need for heating is in practice limited to particularly cold days with cloudy weather. **Ventilation:** The hall has on-demand natural ventilation, with vents controlled by CO_2- and temperature sensors. The service building has balanced mechanical ventilation. **Other measures:** No cooling has been installed in the building. The hall has a cast concrete floor, and is only insulated around the edges. The floor therefore helps to ensure even temperatures throughout the day. In summer, the temperature is kept down by means of forced ventilation through the doorways.

13 GJERDRUM SECONDARY SCHOOL GJERDRUM

KRISTIN JARMUND ARKITEKTER

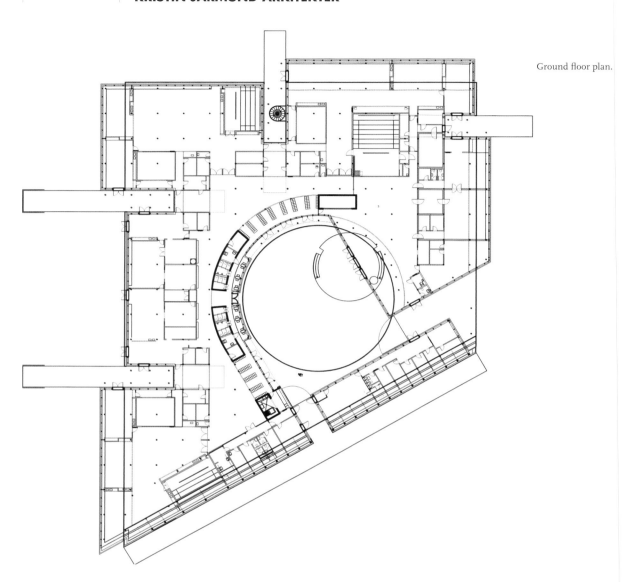

Ground floor plan.

The social life of pupils and teachers are an essential part of learning. Gjerdrum school allows for flexibility and free interaction both inside and out.

The project was the winning entry in an invited competition in 2007. It is designed for four parallel groups, years 8-10, a total of 320 pupils, organised within one compact volume. In this way you get short circulation distances and a plan practically without corridors, with lots of opportunity for social contact in the inner landscape of the school. The centre of the building is the open school "square". A large, circular cut in the roof plane gives daylight and air to the square and the adjoining rooms. A tilted south-facing wall has integrated seating next to the outdoor sports arena.

There is a great variation of spaces within the plan, with open surfaces as well as spaces kept within distinct volumes. Each year has its own area of the plan, but flexibility allows for a great variation of uses. Parts of the school can be separated off and hired out to the local community for evening use. Some of the rooms are "inverted" – exterior atria, cuts in the main volume for outdoor teaching and to aid daylight penetration. These atria are also connected with the surrounding landscaping as "piers". Adjacent to each of these atria is a ventilation tower covered in coloured glass.

Universal access has been given priority. Contrast between different surfaces and furnishing elements and the provision of lead lines are some of the interior features. Materiality and colour scheme has also been adapted to aid orientation.

Kristin Jarmund Arkitekter

PROJECT INFORMATION:
Project title: Gjerdrum Secondary School. **Address:** Brådalsgutua, Gjerdrum.
Completed: 2009. **Client:** Gjerdrum Municipality. **Architect:** Kristin Jarmund
Arkitekter. **Team:** Kristin Jarmund, Geir Messel, Arild Eriksen, Francis
Brekke, Nora Müller and Karin Anton. **Interior architect:** Kristin Jarmund
Arkitekter. **Landscape architect:** Østengen & Bergo. **Gross area:** approx. 4000
sq.m. **Costs ex VAT:** NOK 108 million. **Photos:** Rune Stokmo.

ENVIRONMENTAL INFORMATION: Estimated energy consumption:
121 kWh/sq.m. per year. **Gross area per user:** 11,1 sq.m. **Average U-value (W/
sq.m.K):** Walls: 0.16, roof: 0.10, floor: 0.11, glazing: 1.10, area of glazing:
15.7% of gross heated area. **Energy sources:** Electric boiler/district heating.
Ventilation: Decentralised mechanical for more efficient control. **Materials:**
Maintenance free materials where possible. Timber is impregnated pine,
facades toughened glass, natural stone and exposed concrete. Floor coverings
linoleum.

14 OUTDOOR FIREPLACE TRONDHEIM

HAUGEN/ZOHAR ARKITEKTER

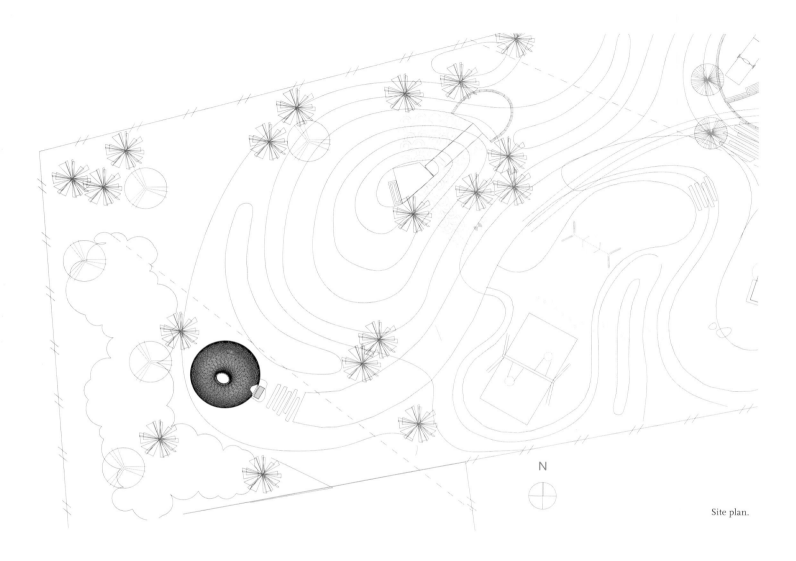

N

Site plan.

Outdoor play is a central part of a Norwegian childhood. This unusual construction gives room for gatherings and stories around an open fire.

Haugen/Zohar were invited by the Municipality of Trondheim to provide a proposal for an outdoor project for a kindergarten.

The architects wanted to combine the usual playground facilities with a room that provided shelter from the weather, for bonfires, storytelling and play. The budget was extremely limited, and the design is based on a structure built of short planks, recycled materials from a building site in the neighbourhood. The inspiration was derived from the old Norwegian turf huts and log cabins, and the little timber construction consists of 80 circles in layers placed on top of each other on an illuminated concrete platform. The circles have different radiuses, and are displaced in relation to each other. Each circle consists of 28 pieces of naturally impregnated pine heartwood, placed at varying distances in order to achieve a chimney effect and natural lighting. Oak spacers create varying vertical distances between the pine planks and ensure air throughflow so that the pine planks are able to dry out. A double-curved sliding door makes it possible to close off and lock the fireplace.

Haugen/Zohar

PROJECT INFORMATION: Outdoor fireplace. **Client:** Trondheim Municipality. **Address:** Trondheim. **Completed:** 2009. **Architect:** Haugen/Zohar Arkitekter. **Contractor:** Pan Landskap. **Photos:** Jason Havneraas and Grethe Fredriksen.

15 THE GEOPARK STAVANGER
HELEN & HARD

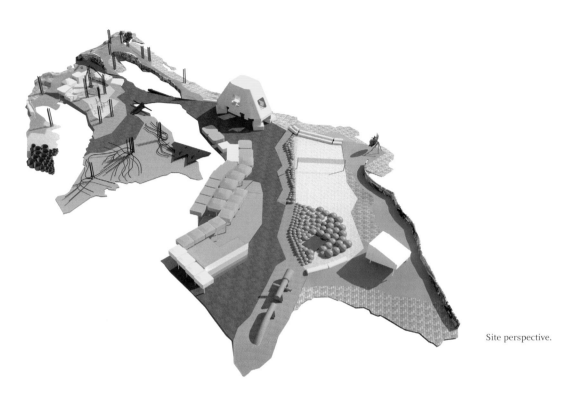

Site perspective.

The oil industry has provided Norway with immeasurable wealth in recent decades. Helen & Hard has made use of industry debris in this public playpark.

Stavanger, the administrative centre of the Norwegian petroleum industry, has during the last 40 years accumulated significant physical and knowledge-based resources around the harvesting, processing and distribution of oil and gas. The urgent challenges of this industry has ignored reflection on a broader application of these resources.

Transferring the resources originally developed for the production of fossil energy to other fields of knowledge, and the engineering of more ecological and humane environments, has been a point of departure for several of Helen & Hard's projects, including the Geopark.

The Geopark directly applies three different types of resource. First, the industry's geological and seismic expertise, second, it's production and handling of technology, materials and waste related to offshore-platforms, and third, the ideas of several youth groups and young individuals for a future park in the city centre.

An interaction between these resource groups and Helen & Hard resulted in a 2500 sq.m. waterfront youth-park and outdoor science centre for the adjacent Norwegian Petroleum Museum.

An initial intention was to give a tangible experience of the oil and gas reservoir "Troll", hidden 2000 – 3000 metres below the seabed. The geological strata and associated drilling and production technology, reconstructed in a scale of 1:500, gives the outlines of the primary topography for Geopark.

This "geo-landscape" is further developed in a sequence of playful and empirical steps, and programmed in workshops with youth groups for various activities like biking, climbing, exhibition, concerts, jumping, ball play and "chill-out" areas. The oil layer in the Troll field, with its drilling wells, is represented as a skating park, and the geological folds are reused as exhibition walls for graffiti and street art. The surfaces and installations are reconstructed out of recycled and reshaped elements from the petroleum installations, the abandoned Frigg platform, offshore bases, equipment suppliers and scrap heaps.

The park is thriving. Kids, parents and youngsters are using the park at all hours, turning a formerly abandoned site into a humming social meeting point. Local newspapers, politicians and park users are now fighting to make the park, which was originally planned as temporary, a permanent feature.

Helen & Hard

PROJECT INFORMATION: The Geopark. **Address:** Kjerringholmen, Stavanger. **Completed:** 2008. **Client:** Stavanger 2008, European Capital of Culture. **Architects:** Helen&Hard. **Team:** Siv Helene Stangeland, Reinhard Kropf, Randi Hana Augenstein, Barbara Ascher, Dag Strass, Mercedes Pena, Robert Reichkendler. Developed in collaboration with Norwegian Petroleum Museum. **Gross area:** 2448 sq.m. **Cost ex. vat:** NOK 5 362 500. **Photos:** Emilie Ashley, Tom Haga and Helen & Hard.

ENVIRONMENTAL INFORMATION: Surfaces and installations are built from recycled and redesigned materials from the petroleum industry, gathered from decomissioned oil rigs, offshore bases, equipment suppliers and scrapyards.

...
The white house
where she couldn't live,
the balcony, the gate,
and the print in the newspaper when she disappeared.
...

Tone Hødnebø

THE PRIVATE
CHALLENGE

Architecture expresses our aspirations, they way we want to live. In private projects, the clients get to shape their environments to reflect their attitudes to home and family life, to the surrounding social environment, to local expectations and resources, and to the landscape.

Main level plan.

At the edge of a farm at Rennesøy outside Stavanger, this modest house makes use of the ruins of a pigsty as the foundation for a new structure.

The setting has a number of distinctive qualities – large trees, stone walls, a grassy slope, rocks reminiscent of Japanese gardens and a view of the sea. The new farmhouse has been placed approximately 150 metres from the existing farm buildings so as not to disturb the original cluster of old buildings. The starting point is the old pigsty, which provides room for rough functions such as the store room and the entrance to the laundry. The new dwelling volume has been placed above ground. The floor area is small, only 118 sq.m., and the house has been built with a very limited budget. The plan is simple: a cross in the middle of the rectangle contains storage space, bathroom and entrance. The middle of the cross is shifted in order to give the kitchen and living room greater depth than the four bedrooms. Despite of the modest floor area, the plan allows several circulation patterns. The body of the house resembles a tunnel, open at both ends, so that the house appears symmetrical while the setting contrasts with this symmetry, intimate at one side and wide open at the other. The ceiling height has been raised in both the kitchen and the living room.

The house is mainly prefabricated. Timber slab technology has been used in floors, walls and ceilings. Prefabricated elements in whitewood have been left untreated. The cores have been built in a conventional manner and painted black.

Knut Hjeltnes

PROJECT INFORMATION: Farmhouse Dalaker/Galta. **Address:** Dalaker, Rennesøy. **Completed:** 2005. **Client:** Turi Dalaker, Tom Galta. **Architect:** Knut Hjeltnes. **Gross area:** 150.3 sq.m. **Photos:** Nils Petter Dale.

ENVIRONMENTAL INFORMATION: Built area: 37.6 sq.m. per resident. **Average U-value:** For walls/ceiling/floor 0.16 W/sq.m.K; for windows 1.2 W/sq.m.K. **Energy sources:** Wood and natural gas. **Ventilation:** Natural.

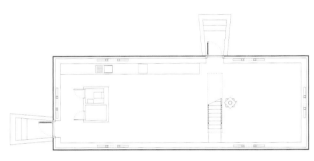

Ground floor plan.

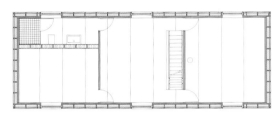

First floor plan.

The inexpensive site in the middle of a housing development seemed to have little to offer residents. But in cooperation with the architects, the owners made some bold and surprising choices.

The villa was designed for a young couple with two small children, who wanted wood and glass to be the main materials of their new house. The site is in the middle of a housing development on the outskirts of Trondheim, and was less expensive than many of the neighbouring properties since it lacks a direct view of the Trondheim Fjord. Three sides of the site border on neighbouring houses, while the fourth side faces a pretty little copse with brushwood and large trees.

The house is divided horizontally into three parts of very different character: the ground floor, private floor and roof terrace. The ground floor is open and accessible, consisting of a single large, open room, partly set into the ground. This room contains the main entrance, the entrance from the garden, the kitchen, living room, dining room and a small WC. The family can easily regulate the inward and outward views with curtains and a flexible lighting system, but they prefer as a rule to keep the façade open. The compact second floor with its relatively low ceilings has a closed and private character. It contains

bedrooms, rooms for work and recreation and bathrooms. Windows are evenly distributed as openings in the façade.

Thorough studies of the topography showed that a roof terrace would allow this client to enjoy a splendid view of the landscape from all sides, not least towards the Trondheim Fjord. In this way, a relatively inexpensive site was turned into a first class location.

The railing around the roof terrace contains storage space, a refrigerator, a stereo system, a grill, water supply and power points.

The top half of the house is constructed as a stiff "box" of solid wooden elements. It stands on six slender steel pillars, triangulated so as to take wind stresses. The house has balanced ventilation with air-to-air heat recovery, a geothermal heat pump for heating rooms and water and a wood stove.

Brendeland & Kristoffersen

PROJECT INFORMATION: Villa Borgen/Nilsen. **Address:** Humlehaug-veien 32, Trondheim. **Completed:** 2008. **Client:** Linda Borgen and Nikolai Nilsen. **Architect:** Brendeland & Kristoffersen arkitekter. **Team:** Geir Brendeland, Olav Kristoffersen, Simen Stori. **Gross area:** 141 sq.m. **Photos:** Ivan Brodey.

ENVIRONMENTAL INFORMATION: Energy consumption: Not calculated. **Built area:** 35 sq.m. per resident. **Average U-value:** Ceiling 0.13 W/sq.m.K; outer wall: 0.21 W/sq.m.K; ground floor: 0.12 W/sq.m.K; windows: 1.1 W/sq.m.K. **Energy sources:** Geothermal heating of rooms and water, wood stove **Ventilation:** Balanced ventilation with rotating heat recovery.

18 CABIN VARDEHAUGEN ÅFJORD

FANTASTIC NORWAY

Ground floor plan.

On a flat rock by the Atlantic Ocean, Fantastic Norway has created their version of the traditional "cluster yard" in a solution that combines the panoramic view with shelter from the wild weather.

The coastal cabin has been placed on Vardehaugen, an outcrop of rock by the mouth of the fjord on the Fosen peninsula in Trøndelag.

The project is a result of the client's wish for a cabin to suit the needs of the family, the distinctive site and the shifting climate of the area. The site is located 35 metres above sea level in a small depression with panoramic vistas in three directions. The building is inspired by the traditional Norwegian cluster yard, where flexible sheltered outdoor spaces and a clear social organisation are the main principles.

The body of the building lies snugly along a low mountain ridge, hugging the polished rock. The kitchen is the backbone of the building, tying the different rooms together. Here one has an overview of the cabin and the atrium, and access to the panoramic view out to sea. The bedrooms and the bathroom are located at the back of the house and the living room furthest out, like an observatory. The plan is open, but has nooks and crannies where one can enjoy a little privacy.

To provide maximum protection for the cabin, the black roof is folded down to become a wall on the sides most exposed to the weather. The wall surfaces are angled to prevent the wind from taking hold. By the entrance and the living spaces the rough dark walls are replaced by horizontal white panelling. The cabin is constructed with a simple timber frame, clad with impregnated pine. The cabin is anchored with steel cables that extend from the ground beam via the foundation wall to the bedrock.

Fantastic Norway

PROJECT INFORMATION: Atrium cabin on Vardehaugen. **Address:** Grøttingen, Åfjord. **Completed:** 2008. **Client:** Knut Aasarød and Synnøve Matre. **Architect:** Fantastic Norway (Håkon Matre Aasarød). **Interior:** Sigrid Bjørkum. **Gross area:** 77 sq.m. **Photos:** Arne Michal Paulsen and Sveinung Bråthen.

ENVIRONMENTAL INFORMATION: Built area: Approximately 15 sq.m. per resident. **Energy sources:** Primary: electricity; secondary: passive solar heat, wood stove. **Ventilation:** Natural. **Other measures:** Separate greywater treatment system, outer walls, ceilings and floor are well insulated and windows are double-glazed.

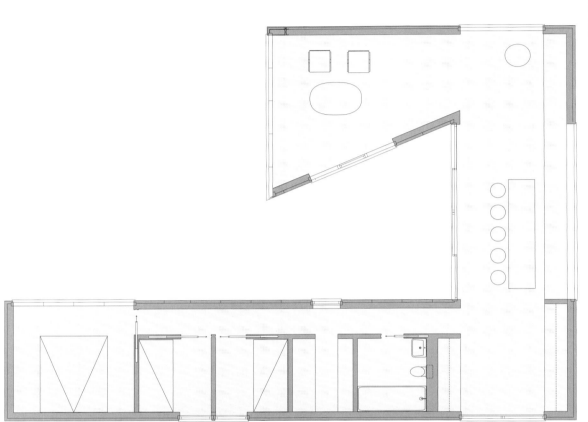

Ground floor plan.

A Norwegian summer house is traditionally a modest structure, set in spectacular surroundings. This cabin is pared down to the bare necessities of living.

The design of a holiday cabin is pared down to the bare necessities of living. Life moves in a circle from one simple task to another, and the programme is a basic one: cooking, eating, sleeping, washing, being together. The design is correspondingly basic – the architectonic result follows this limited programme and is tailored to the direction, climate and topography of the landscape.

The site lies in the skerries on the outermost point of Papperøy Island in the municipality of Hvaler, one of Norway's most popular summer holiday locations. It consists of a plateau in an archipelago landscape that varies from deep rocky clefts to flat areas with low vegetation. The plateau is situated 25 metres above sea level, exposed to the wind and with a panoramic view of the sea and the horizon.

The cabin is a slim building with small rooms – the inside is always close to the outside. It is organised around a courtyard, making the outside inside. This produces a sequence of spaces, one behind the other: from the inside we look onto the outside, which looks into a further inside space, which looks onto yet another outside space.

The building stands on piles directly on the rock and consists of a wooden structure with cross-bracing steel elements. It is clad with horizontal oak boards of heartwood fixed with acid-proof screws, and all the exterior terraces are made of larch wood. The interior surfaces are clad with untreated birch: plywood for the ceilings and walls and solid wood for the floors. Energy saving glass has been used. Areas of glazing that are not meant to be opened are merely mounted with sealant.

Reiulf Ramstad Arkitekter

PROJECT INFORMATION: Cabin Inside-Out. **Location:** Papperhavn, Hvaler. **Client:** Sofie, August and Kristin Ramstad. **Architect:** Reiulf Ramstad Arkitekter. **Team:** Reiulf Ramstad, Anders Tjønneland. **Consultant:** Walter Jacobsen, engineer. **Gross area:** 74 sq.m. **Photo:** Kim Müller.

ENVIRONMENTAL INFORMATION: The cabin is used in spring, summer and autumn, and is insulated accordingly. It is heated by solar power alone and has natural ventilation.

20 | HOUSING, STØPERIGATEN 25 STAVANGER
ALLIANCE ARKITEKTER

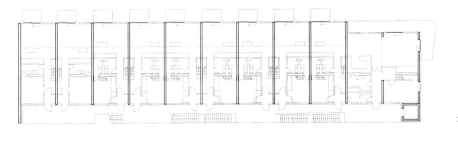

Second floor plan.

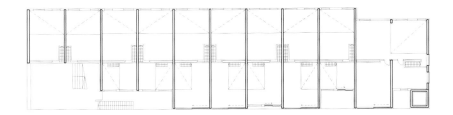

Second floor plan, mezzanine level.

Støperigaten 25 is a modern and playful condominium in the centre of Stavanger with an emphasis on good daylight, high ceilings, flexible dwellings and active communal zones.

The building was originally planned for first-time buyers and younger home buyers. However, the design of the apartments proved to be an answer to challenges involved in facilitating more flexible solutions in a longer perspective than is normal in relation to the size of the apartments. The room solutions and design details are simple, so the residents can alter and upgrade the dwelling themselves.

The planning began with the outdoor areas. The roof terrace, the broad access galleries, the play areas and the passage through the block are designed with regard for the way the building relates to the urban fabric around it and to the public spaces. A common laundry and a common room for the residents have been incorporated into the ground floor, with a door out to a small play area to the north. The common room will be available to residents for meetings and other social activities.

All of the apartments have an open mezzanine over the living room. Most of them also have a mezzanine over the bedroom. The ceiling height of the apartments is up to 4.5 metres, and the open mezzanines provide additional space. Some bedrooms have an en-suite bathroom and minikitchen, which makes them suitable for letting out. All of the apartments have a south-west oriented balcony or terrace. The façade facing the street is designed with open approaches, cantilevered open lofts and steps leading directly from the pavement to the roof terrace. Galleries vary in width, and it is possible for the residents to furnish common meeting places on the galleries, facing the street. The façades to the north and west are designed to be in keeping with the neighbouring buildings, and have a more conventional expression, with white-painted panelling and vertical windows.

Alliance Arkitekter

PROJECT INFORMATION: Housing «Innbo». **Address:** Støperigaten 25, Stavanger. **Completed:** 2007. **Client:** Svithun Invest. **Architect:** Alliance arkitekter. **Team:** Harald Martin Gjøvaag, Kristoffer Johan Gulbrandsen, Tue Kappel, Tonje Løvdahl. **Interior:** Alliance arkitekter. **Landscape:** Alliance arkitekter. **Area:** 3007 sq.m. **Photos:** Stian Robberstad.

ENVIRONMENTAL INFORMATION: The building's energy framework: 81 kWh/m²K/year, **Estimated energy consumption:** 65 kWh/m²K/year. The apartments have been made ready for installation of water-borne heating/underfloor heating. **U-values:** Façade/outer walls: 0.35 W/sq.m.K, roof: 0.17 W/sq.m.K. **Ventilation:** Mechanical evacuation. Fresh air intake through ventilators in outer walls with soundproofing and filtration.

...
You are walking

on the outside of the forest, knee high

in ferns.

Feeling how

everything earthly

gathers

weight.

Under that,

you stay

upright.

...

Tor Ulven

LOCAL
CHALLENGES

Much of Norway is characterised by an extreme climate, and the immediate presence of the untouched natural landscape. The Arctic north, with polar cold and darkness in the winter and midnight sun in the summer, is a strong presence. But local experience also includes history, habits and smaller-scale environments.

21 ARCTIC CULTURE CENTRE HAMMERFEST

A-LAB

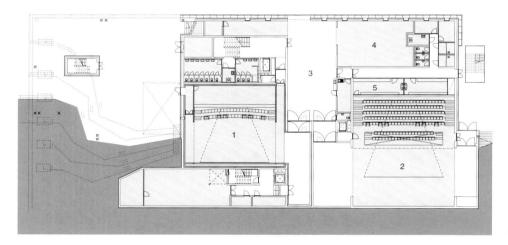

1. Black box/cinema
2. Main stage
3. Workshop
4. Storage
5. Cloakrooms

Ground floor plan.

The Arctic Culture Centre is the first step in the development of a large area along the seafront in Hammerfest town centre, and provides the area with new functions and a distinctive architectural character.

Hammerfest, the world's northernmost town, lies on the coast of northern Norway as a natural centre for the region. Its location close to the North Cape makes the city one of the most important tourist destinations of the area, with over 250 000 visitors each year. The new culture centre is visible both from the sea and from land, adding a major feature to the townscape. An external skin of glass is lit up by LED lighting in the colours of ice and northern lights through the long, dark winters. In summer, the lights are turned off, and the "Hammerfest-red" wooden panelling is visible behind the glass.

The culture centre is organised in compact units, creating spaces with different degrees of public access. Internal and external public areas form social arenas that link the centre to Hammerfest town. In keeping with the principles of the proposed town plan, whereby public spaces are to connect the town with the water, the foyer is expressed as an open, climati-sed public space between Strandgata and the quay. "The Arctic Arena", an outdoor auditorium, is conceptually like the other spaces that connect the main street with the North Sea, but this public space does not lie between buildings, but under a cantilevered volume. It forms the start (or end) of the development and is the face of the centre towards the town.

Transparent façades reveal the activities within the building, which, while meeting the requirements regarding professional dramatic art and cinema, is also an open and accessible location for many different users. Universal design and accessibility for all members of the public has been important. To help visually impaired persons, there are directional guide lines in the floors in public areas. Walls and doors are colour-coded.

a-lab

PROJECT INFORMATION: Arctic Culture Centre. **Address:** Strandgata 32, 9600 Hammerfest. **Completed:** 2009. **Client:** Hammerfest local authority. **Architect:** A-lab (Arkitekturlaboratoriet) (Adnan Harambasic). **Interior architect (pilot project):** Zinc (Heide Tjøm & Guri Mo). **Interior (design-build contract):** A-lab. **Landskapsarkitekt:** Remark! (Mona Kramer Wendelborg). **Gross area:** 5000 sq.m. **Photos:** Ivan Brodey.

ENVIRONMENTAL INFORMATION: Estimated energy consumption: 140 kWh/sq.m/year. **Average U-value:** 0.36 W/sq.m.K. **Energy sources:** Variable volume oil-fired, made ready for gas.

22 | PETTER DASS MUSEUM ALSTAHAUG

SNØHETTA

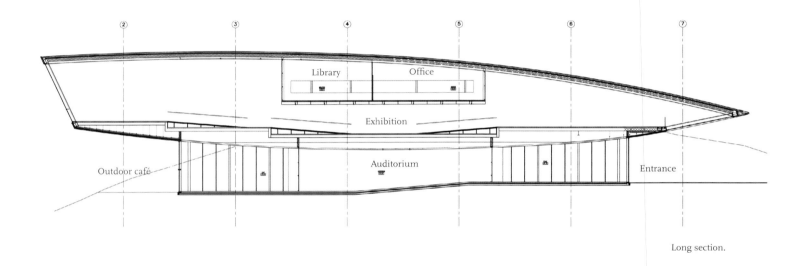

Long section.

The poet-preacher Peter Dass' peaceful parsonage at Alstahaug in northern Norway, with a history dating back to the 18th century, has a new neighbour, cut into the rock and overlooking the sea.

Alstahaug municipality in Nordland county is known for its magnificent landscape, bordered by the mountain range "The Seven Sisters" on one side and on the other 1200 islands and skerries, which have given it the name "kingdom of a thousand islands". The Petter Dass Museum is situated in the grounds of a long-established church 20 kilometres from the town of Sandnessjøen. The site consists of a church, a churchyard, a parsonage and several other buildings including the original museum, which was opened in 1966. This has now been extended by a new museum building and parking facilities that were designed by Snøhetta in 2007.

The parsonage was the home of the Norwegian poet Petter Dass, who was parson of Alstahaug from 1689 to 1707, although the present 18th-century parsonage was built some years later. The complex and its surroundings are a popular recreational area for both tourists and the local population, and the museum is a national documentation and resource centre based on Petter Dass and his significant position in Norwegian and Nordic cultural history.

Snøhetta was responsible for the project from 2001 until its completion. The aim was to design a new museum building, a landscape plan for the surrounding site, parking facilities and a service building. During the process the architect rejected the site proposed by the client on the grounds that building a new museum there would deflect attention away from the historic surroundings. Instead a cut was made in the rocky landscape west of the church and a freestanding building constructed between the two wire-cut rock walls. The new museum thus respects the historic site and serves as a visual expression of the historical span between the date when the church was built and the present.

Snøhetta

PROJECT INFORMATION: Petter Dass Museum. **Address:** Alstahaug, Sandnessjøen. **Completed:** 2007. **Client:** KF Petter Dass Eiendom. **Architect:** Snøhetta. **Team:** Kjetil T. Thorsen, Tarald Lundevall, Astrid Renata Van Veen, Maria Svaland, Jim Dodson, Bartosz Milewski, Tom Holtmann, Ellen Heier, Andreas Nygaard. **Interior architect:** Snøhetta: Heidi Pettersvold. **Landscape architects:** Snøhetta: Jenny B. Osuldsen, Lars Jørstad Nordbye. **Consultants:** Frank Jacobsen, Norconsult, VVSplan, Per Rasmussen, Brekke og Strand. **Gross area:** 1350 sq.m. **Cost exclusive of VAT:** NOK 38,7 million (contract sum for the service and museum buildings and the landscape plan). **Photos:** Åke E. Lindman.

EXPERTISE AND INTUITION

INTERVIEW | **KJETIL TRÆDAL THORSEN, PARTNER, SNØHETTA**
BY JAN CARLSEN

It's tempting to call Snøhetta a fantastic success story. At the same time, it should be noted that Snøhetta's remarkable rise to success is based on devotion to the profession, a collective way of working and a genuine belief in the importance of good architecture. Architect Kjetil Trædal Thorsen, who trained at the Graz University of Technology in Austria, graduating in 1985, is one of the partners and original founders of the firm, which today has over 100 employees in Oslo. He talks about the firm's ideology, organisation and working methods.

JAN CARLSEN: Snøhetta has an international image from more than one point of view, and I'll come back to this, but first I'd like to ask you: Was the basis for this global profile laid as early as 1989? When you were just a small firm, newly established in Oslo, and went to Los Angeles, rented premises and equipment, and designed your entry for the international competition for the new Alexandria Library in Egypt? Which you so sensationally won after a hard battle with architects from all over the world?
KJETIL TRÆDAL THORSEN: We were young and confident and wanted to put ourselves to the test by entering a major international competition, so this was

what you might call a flying start. Until then, we had only come second or third place in competitions and purchases in some national competitions.

We rented a flat consisting of three rooms and a kitchen in downtown LA, and there we worked and ate and slept, and we rented all our drawing equipment from the local film industry. The foundation for Snøhetta was indeed laid

"THE BEST AND MOST POPULAR ARCHITECTURE ALWAYS HAS AN ELEMENT OF SOUND SOCIAL DEMOCRATIC IDEOLOGY."

then, in 1989, but what really counted was our own determination and the help we received in the years after we had won the competition for this legendary library.

JC: One of the other competitors tried to steal the project from under your nose.
KTT: Yes, the Italians were certainly on the offensive; they really wanted the library, and they tried to trick their way to the commission. But thanks to the resolute initiative of several individuals, including Norway's woman prime minister, Gro Harlem Brundtland, the project went to us. But only by a very

slight margin – the project could just as well have gone to the Italians. In the end it was an elegant effort by our supporters that decided the issue.

The Opera House in Oslo was inaugurated about 20 years later. It was these two buildings – these two international victories – that placed Snøhetta on the architectural map. But you have to remember that we didn't suddenly come into the spotlight; it took five years – from the opera competition win in 2000 – before we began attracting so much attention. And then when the Opera was finally completed, and inaugurated in April 2008, we knew we had finally arrived.

JC: In spite of your strong international image, Snøhetta has often been called a modern Norwegian firm. How do you explain this paradox?
KTT: It's not a paradox; Norwegian contemporary architecture is very international. But having said that, the name Snøhetta has played a role, with its associations with Norway's snow-capped mountains and the mighty Dovrefjellet. And also the firm's address is in Oslo – we haven't left the country – we pay our taxes in Norway and are a completely Norwegian private limited company.

Snøhetta offices, Oslo.

PHOTO: MARTE GARMAN JOHNSEN/SNØHETTA

Another factor that enhances our national profile could be the fact that in our projects we seek a unity between architecture and landscape. This interplay between the building and its natural surroundings has helped to shape our identity – this isn't the case in every country.

The accessibility of architecture

JC: What about the social aspects?

KTT: The best and most popular architecture always has an element of sound social democratic ideology; buildings should be as public as possible. In my view, the ideal is a building with many different entrances and unlimited accessibility, like a park.

I'm talking here about the horizontality of architecture, about generosity, openness towards the users. Public buildings take up a lot of ground space, and so they should. The potential inherent in flat architecture has always preoccupied Snøhetta.

JC: You're thinking of how people love being able to walk on the roof of the Oslo Opera House, and the intimate relationship between the building and the water?

KTT: And the Library at Alexandria.

Both these cultural buildings have public functions and we've given them a horizontal, inviting form. They're inclusive. There's a risk that a building can act as a physical barrier, which in turn creates a mental barrier. In Snøhetta we often talk about the unity between body and mind, and this symbiosis is valid both for architecture and for the way it is perceived. One of architecture's most vital characteristics is its sensuality.

JC: In your work, how important are the metaphors from nature that many people associate with your firm, like the parallel between the Opera House and an iceberg?

KTT: People are free to interpret us in

"A BRILLIANT CONCEPT CAN BE HIDDEN IN A CASUAL REMARK OR A SUDDEN LEAP OF ASSOCIATION."

any way they want, it's not up to Snøhetta to decide how the completed building should be perceived. But it would be wrong to say that the design process is driven by such motives. Qualified architecture critics and other professionals should at least know better than that. White marble doesn't automatically ex-

press an iceberg. We could just as easily have been thinking of the smooth rocky slopes on the coast when we decided on the form of the Opera House and the way it fits in with the fjord landscape.

Wait before you put pen to paper

JC: Can you describe the most important creative working methods that Snøhetta uses in the initial conceptual design phases of a project?

KTT: As I mentioned above, we have a special focus on two parameters: Horizontality and an openness in our way of working. The work of an architect is too complex and demanding for one person alone, and that's why we concentrate on team-building and try out different processes of cross-disciplinary cooperation. The keyword is interaction, or "transing", which means transpositioning between different fields of expertise. It's a little like an orchestra where the members exchange instruments during the rehearsals, try out new things, experiment, and then go back to their own instruments when the concert begins. But the whole thing usually starts as group work in a workshop setting. The atmosphere is a mixture of extremely concentrated interaction and hilarious jokes; it's important to loosen the knots that are blocking creativity. You have to be alert the whole time, incredibly focused, and make decisions at the right moment.

JC: And what do you do then?
KTT: There's one particular method we use, and that's before the actual designing starts: We make an in-depth analysis. Sound architectural work requires a high level of expertise. At Snøhetta we try to do a thorough job before we start on the actual design. There's a lot of intense discussion before we draw a single line; and it takes a long time before the design – the aesthetic expression – is decided.

And during this phase it's especially important to be alert, to catch an innovative idea on the wing, because a brilliant concept can be hidden in a casual remark or a sudden leap of association.

Architects' methods have changed a lot during the last 20 to 30 years; the work has become more professionali-

"WE'VE SAID NO FOR ETHICAL REASONS TO A NUMBER OF COMMISSIONS."

sed. The person who produces the first drawing has a lot of influence. That's why we deliberately keep to diagrams in the early phases.

When I was a student working with the architect Ralph Erskine in Stockholm, the situation was completely different. A lot of the design was based on intuition, spontaneous solutions; you arrived at a coherent solution by working through a series of drafts. We don't work like that any more.

JC: After you won the competition for the 11th September pavilion on Ground Zero in 2004, I understand that the social-democratic model was quite difficult to follow in your "Norwegian" branch office in New York, headed by your partner Craig Dykers. Is this correct? Are you an ambassador for exemplary Norwegian working conditions abroad?
KTT: Yes, it's more difficult to run the office in a typically Snøhetta way in the US than it is here at home. For example, it's difficult to get Americans to understand

that you're allowed to take a holiday, to work no more than nine hours a day, take maternity leave and so on. These benefits are self-evident to us Scandinavians, but the people at the New York office have a guilty conscience when they're not at work; they're trained to be at the drawing board around the clock. Our argument is that an architect needs rest, fresh impulses and inspiration, in order to stay creative year after year. Such clashes between cultures can easily arise when you transfer the social-democratic model to other countries.

Reform movements and the work of an architect

JC: Snøhetta's team consists of architects from many different countries. How does this "brotherhood", this cosmopolitan aspect, influence the working environment at the office and the architecture you produce?
KTT: Currently there are around 106 employees from 16 countries, and this ethnic and cultural mix expands everyone's horizon. It makes us better at listening to one another, we pay more attention to each other in this kind of productive fusion. A lot of the dialogue is in English, and this diversity creates a lot of exciting and unexpected connections. The cross-disciplinary composition of the office has the same effect.

JC: You've appointed an ethics council at the office, and you consult for example Amnesty International in certain difficult cases. Can you give some examples of conflicts with professional ethics and other professional issues that can arise when you're working on projects in other countries?
KTT: In principle, working is just as difficult and just as easy almost anywhere in the world. When we're working in a particular country we first try to discover similarities with our own culture, so that we understand the differences better. For example, the US is neither worse nor better in this respect; our American colleagues have high professional integrity and make a great effort to create high-quality, socially responsible architecture.
But there are countries with undemocra-

tic governments, capital punishment, discrimination against women, lack of freedom of expression, and other violations of human rights. Obviously it's easy to get your hands dirty when you

"THE RISK IS THAT IF YOU WORK ONLY WITH COMPUTERS IT RESULTS IN A NARROW STYLE."

take on a project in such conditions. But take Saudi Arabia. Even in that country there are movements to improve social conditions, voices claiming that liberal reforms are in line with Islam. Should we not support such movements? Maybe the changes are only small and gradual under the rule of the conservative Sharia elements, but still one must hope that cooperation and dialogue make a difference.

JC: So architectural activities can have a diplomatic, foreign-policy dimension?
KTT: Refusing all commissions from countries like this would undermine their positive ambitions. But we've had long, intense discussions about this, and if we do refuse to take on a commission we make our reasons very clear. When we agreed to design the Alexandria Library, we were told by a lot of people that Egypt is not a democratic country, that half of its citizens are illiterate and that the costs of the building would make huge inroads in the country's resources. But today the Library's reading rooms are packed, and children and young people have free access to literature and cultural activities. Also this library, which also attracts tourists, has helped both the authorities and public opinion in Egypt to understand more about what can be done through good architecture.

JC: There are huge differences between the desert landscape of Saudi Arabia and the Norwegian mountains and valleys.
KTT: The Saudi Arabians are just as deeply attached to their landscape and their places as we Norwegians are to ours, and this makes it possible to exchange views and share experiences. The problem is that Saudi Arabia is a young nation that

Above: Kapsarc, Saudi Arabia, competition project. Right, top: Ras-al-Khaimah
Gateway project. Right, bottom: Darat King Abdullah II project, Amman.
ILLUSTRATIONS: MIR

has skipped the civilising era of industrialism; the country went straight from a nomadic culture to an information society, and of course this has created an enormous generation gap. Obviously, with this kind of polarisation the ethical complications can be serious.

On the other hand, we've said no for ethical reasons to a number of commissions. For example, the NATO headquarters in Brussels, Belgium, and the military museum in Abu Dhabi, although the reasons were different.

The challenge of China
JC: Would Snøhetta consider a commission in China to be a stimulating challenge?
KTT: If it was the right project, we would say an unconditional yes, it would be a pleasure. We've already received invitations from China, but the time

schedules were too tight and we had to say no. They were in large cities that were expanding rapidly, and obviously in these cases a project is sometimes based on rushed decisions and unpromising conditions from an architectural point of view.

But China is a fantastic country, I've been there many times. So it would be a great honour for a Norwegian firm of architects to have the opportunity to design a major project in the Middle Kingdom.

JC: Do you think there are any questions I haven't asked in this interview?
KTT: You could ask: "What are your plans for the future?"

JC: What are your plans for the future?
KTT: We want to further develop a concept we started about 20 years ago,

when we were designing the Alexandria library: Increasing the breadth of expertise of our staff and concentrating on more workshop-oriented production. I'm thinking of the possibility of combining digital and analogue processes. The challenge for architects today is to extend their working methods from computers to physical, tactile objects, for example by modelling and prototyping. We have to start using a lot of different tools and not get stuck in digital working methods.

The risk is that if you work only with computers it results in a narrow style because predictable design is inherent in this tool. We must be brave enough and innovative enough to examine all the creative possibilities in the repertoire of our profession.

Jan Carlsen

23 | HOUSING, BJØRNVEIEN 119 OSLO

DAHLE / DAHLE / BREITENSTEIN

Entrance level plan.

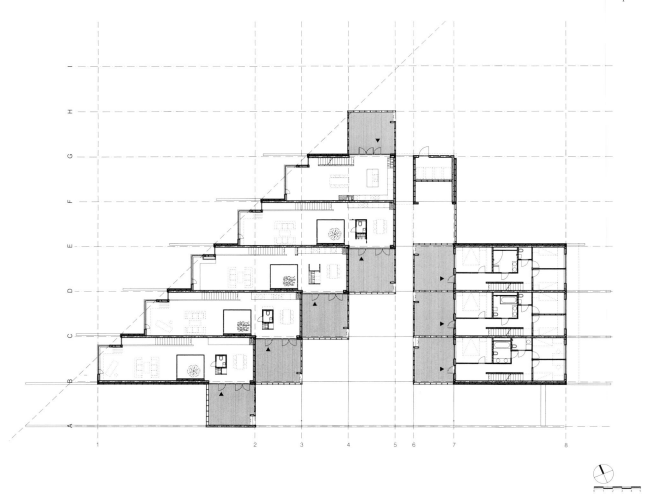

Community, flexibility, sustainability and light. These inventive row houses in a low-density suburb of Oslo meet a range of different needs.

Bjørnveien 119 is situated in an area of large one-family and multifamily houses, close to a sports ground and a petrol station.

The project has been conceived as a compact complex with the scale of a small-house development. It consists of four two-storey patio houses, two of 154 sq.m. and two of 130 sq.m., one west-facing house of 161 sq.m. with veranda, and three three-storey, east-facing houses of 136 sq.m. with balconies. Between the two lines of buildings lies a communal courtyard, with parking beneath. The complex is a synthesis of qualities borrowed from the detached house, the row house, and the apartment. The rooms within each unit are versatile and can be adapted to changing needs. All units have three outside spaces: a front garden leading to the main entrance, a back

lawn, and a veranda, balcony or patio, depending on the type of house. In several units a two-storey well with glass on three sides extends upwards from the lowest level, allowing the inhabitants to appreciate the various seasons, with their sun, rain, snow, from indoors. One of the main goals was to ensure that light enters the houses from all angles.

The houses are built in in-situ concrete, insulated and faced with narrow black-painted wooden boards, horizontal on the long facades and upright on the short facades. They rely on "green" energy, and 100-sq.m. of solar collector panels are mounted on the south-facing facade. All floors have a waterborne underfloor heating system, supplemented by a gas heater.

Dahle / Dahle / Breitenstein

PROJECT INFORMATION: Housing Bjørnveien 119. **Address:** Bjørnveien 119, Oslo. **Completed:** 2005. **Client:** Backe Prosjekt. **Architect:** Dahle / Dahle / Breitenstein (now Einar Dahle Arkitekter and Dahle & Breitenstein). **Team:** Einar Dahle, Christian Dahle and Kurt Breitenstein, Joachim Dahle og Christine Engh, stud. arch., Ane Maja Sollid, stud. ing. **Gross area:** 1 868 sq.m., including garages. **Cost exclusive of VAT:** NOK 21.1 million. **Photos:** Nils Petter Dale.

ENVIRONMENTAL INFORMATION: Energy consumption: Approx. 100 000 kWh/year or about 100 kWh/sq.m. living area/year. **Land use:** 35–45 sq.m./person excluding garages. **Average U value:** 0.21 W/sq.m. **Energy sources:** Solar, gas and electricity. **Ventilation:** Hybrid. **Energy system:** 100 sq.m. solar collector panels combined with 2 x 24 kW gas boilers. Distributed as low-temperature water-borne underfloor heating and hot tap water. The solar collector is expected to produce around 270 kWh/sq.m. panel.

24 | YPSILON BRIDGE DRAMMEN
ARNE EGGEN ARKITEKTER

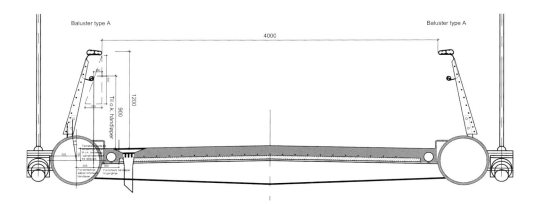

The connectivity offered by a new pedestrian bridge is an important part of a new urbanising strategy for Drammen.

The municipality of Drammen, which occupies a central position south-west of Oslo, has in the last few years put a great deal of work into developing and upgrading their urban environment, with dynamic results. Geographically, the centre of Drammen is divided in two, with the urban districts of Bragernes and Strømsø on either bank of the beautiful Drammenselva river.

A new bridge has become an important visual element linking the pedestrian routes on either side. The main principle of the design was to integrate the bridge into the river landscape and limit the impact on the surrounding environment.

The Bragernes bank is a popular place from which to view the river and the town. The Y-shaped plan of the bridge, which splits into two arms as it reaches the shore, has preserved the small inlet on this bank as a landscape space. The Y-shape also provides extra length and height to the span, providing a

free navigable height under the bridge of 6 x 15 metres, and giving a user-friendly gradient that satisfies the requirements of universal design.

The bridge has a main span of 90 metres with a 4-metre wide steel deck, and two 45-metre side spans, each with a 3-metre steel deck. It is entirely supported by cables attached to two 47-metre towers. The towers and the double side spans provide good lateral stiffness and stability. All the steel parts are painted white and the deck is paved with crushed white granite embedded in resin.

The steel structure was produced by a steelworks in Sandnessjøen and transported down the coast by sea. The construction was carried out by free extension of the elements of the main span in 10-metre lengths towards the anchor on the Strømsø side.

Arne Eggen Arkitekter

PROJECT INFORMATION: Ypsilon pedestrian and cycling bridge.
Location: Drammen. **Completed:** 2008. **Client:** Drammen municipality.
Architect: Arne Eggen Arkitekter. **Team:** Arne Eggen (project leader), Nanna Meidel, Mira Refsum, Karin Hagen and Helge Aarstad. **Landscape architect:** Multiconsult, Seksjon 13.3 landscape architects. **Cost excl. VAT:** NOK 63 million. **Photos:** Terje Løchen, Kaare M. Skallerud and Arne Eggen Arkitekter.

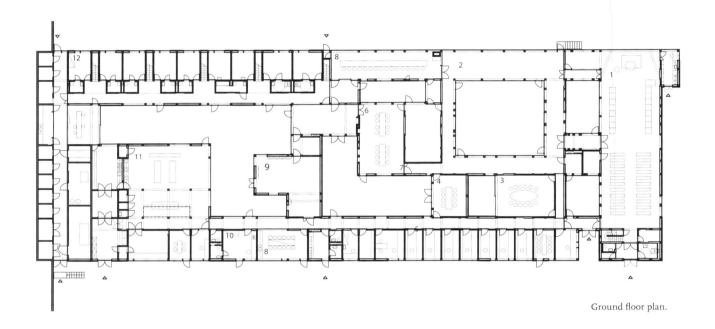

Ground floor plan.

The simple spaces of the convent on Tautra inspires calm and insight, enhanced by the meeting with the immediate landscape and the dramatic scenery beyond.

On the island of Tautra in the Trondheim Fjord lies a new convent for eighteen nuns. It contains a small church and all the necessary facilities for the nuns' life and work. The clients are nuns from various countries, all members of the Cistercian order, who have gathered to realise the vision of creating a new convent precisely here. The ruins of an earlier Cistercian convent, founded in 1207, already lie elsewhere on the island.

An important aspect of the convent as an institution is the nuns' contemplative life. This has had consequences for the architecture. One of the first ideas was to create a low building with a number of gardens that would provide light and create a feeling of seclusion while at the same time opening up the magnificent view across the fjord. Through the glass wall of the refectory, they have a view of the sea and the mountains behind. The convent functions in such a way that, when one of the main rooms is in use, all of the nuns are usually gathered

there. The remaining rooms can then be used as passageways. Most of the rooms occur only once in the plan, and have to fulfil a variety of requirements. A system of rooms with overlapping corners together form seven separate enclosed gardens. Modules are almost only reiterated in the plan when rooms have the same function, such as the private cells. Owing to the varying room sizes, this has resulted in a rather complex plan.

The main structure of the building is of laminated spruce, framed in with laminated timber beams. The covering of Norwegian slates functions rather like a raincoat. The nuns have been active clients, and have planned several parts of the convent themselves, including the landscaping and fencing around the property as well as the design of the seven gardens. This has been done with the help of specialist craftsmen and people from the local parish.

Jensen & Skodvin

PROJECT INFORMATION: Cistercian convent, Tautra.
Address: Tautra, Frosta. **Completed:** 2006. **Client:** Tautra Mariakloster.
Architect: Jensen & Skodvin Arkitektkontor. **Team:** Jan Olav Jensen (project manager), Børre Skodvin, Anne Lise Bjerkan, Torstein Koch, Torunn Golberg, Martin Draleke, Aslak Hanshuus, Kaja Poulsen, Siri Moseng, Minna Riska.
Gross area: 2200 sq.m. **Awards:** Forum AID Award 2007; Selected work, Mies van der Rohe prize for Architecture 2006; Building of the Year 2006; Marmomac International Stone Award 2007. **Photos:** Jensen & Skodvin.

ENVIRONMENTAL INFORMATION: Estimated energy consumption: 180 kWh/sq.m./year. **Built area:** Approx. 120 sq.m./per resident (incl. work areas and church). **Energy sources:** Heat pump (seawater), water-borne floor heating. **Ventilation:** Natural/mechanical.

26 NATIONAL TOURIST ROUTES

Eighteen stretches of road that wind through the most picturesque landscapes of Norway have been designated as National Tourist Routes. They twist and stretch through wild mountain landscapes and forests, and along beautiful fjords, waterfalls and idyllic coastal scenes. These routes have been equipped with new facilities, designed by some of the country's most interesting architects.

The National Tourist Routes present places and traces from history and culture, contrasted with new and surprising architecture, art and landscape design, boosting the nature of Norway as a brand in itself.

Tourism is closely tied to the creative economy, and the aim of the Norwegian Public Roads Administration, who is responsible for the development of the tourist routes, is to strengthen Norway's reputation as travel destination. An important spin-off effect is of course positive growth in local businesses and local communities. The road development is done in close collaboration with architects and landscape architects, and there is a strong emphasis on commissioning young offices, new talents as well as more established names. So far, 40 different architects and landscape architects have been involved. Two architectural advisory boards are involved, to secure best-case projects throughout.

Developing the National Tourists Routes depends on extensive teamwork and active participation from many interested parties, including local municipalities, public institutions, businesses and organisations. Centrally, several different ministries and national institutions are involved. The success of all these overlapping efforts is expressed in the variety of unique road stretches, stopping- and viewpoints highlighting breathtaking natural features. Each project invites visitors who might otherwise never have stepped out of their car, to take part in a fuller experience of the landscape.

The aesthetic challenges are unique to every project, and are resolved differently in each situation according to the particular surroundings in the different terrains and topographies where the routes are established.

Within the project period 2002-2015, almost 2,3 billion Norwegian kroner are to be spent on improving or developing the eighteen tourist routes, comprising 270 upgraded stopping points along 1650 kilometres of road.

Ed.

VIEWPOINT GUDBRANDSJUVET, 2007-2009
VALLDAL/TROLLSTIGEN, GEIRANGER
ARCHITECT: JENSEN & SKODVIN ARKITEKTKONTOR

Gudbrandsjuvet is a series of wild water-falls and pools – created by the river Valldøla, also running through a narrow gorge. According to folktales, this is whe-re Gudbrand jumped across the river, carrying his bride, whom he had stolen from someone else. The area, situated in the north-western area of Norway, is an attraction, reaching 250 000 visitors every summer. Jensen & Skodvins work makes the gorge accessible and safe, by encircling a small hillock in a steel and concrete structure with a slender steel railing.

PHOTO: RUNE GROV AND HELGE SCHJELDERUP

HIKING PATH, SVANDALSFOSSEN, 2006
SAUDA–ROPEID, RYFYLKE
ARCHITECT: HAGA & GROV WITH HELGE SCHJELDERUP

This stopping point presents the experience of the Svandalsfossen waterfall, which lies on a National Tourist route between the small industrial city of Sauda and the village of Ropeid, along the north-western side of the Saudafjord. The project allows safe crossing of the road and a wet and wild "next to nature" experience.

On one side, the road is widened to allow for parking, and from there a stairway descends to a platform under the road bridge, close to the waterfall itself. Further steel stairs and paths continue down to the fjord. A side arm of the waterfall is reached across a smaller corten steel bridge, where a path leads right to the top.

PHOTO: CARL-VIGGO HØLMEBAKK

REST AREA, STRØMBU, 2008-2009
RONDANE, ATNASJØ, FOLLDAL
ARCHITECT: CARL-VIGGO HØLMEBAKK

The tourist route stretches along the eastern side of the mountain massive of Rondane, where this new rest area functions both as an important trailhead for hikers, as well as a natural stopping point and information centre for car tourists.

The building consists of two parts, a heated shelter and toilet facilities. Bet-ween the two lies the information kiosk. The shelter opens up towards north, with views out to the river and the forest. The buildings are constructed in in-situ concrete. Railings are made from steel, doors and windows from pine wood. The facilites have high emphasis on universal design.

...
The earth turns.
It was an orb of glass
which you licked, which wasn't yours
and inside it is a story
that kept you awake.
...

Tone Hødnebø

GLOBAL
CHALLENGES

While it may not be the case that the world is getting smaller, there is no escaping that the global community affects architecture at least as much as any local context. Politics, finance, industrial practices, technology, climate concerns, forms and ideas – all these and more are part of the background conditions that shape architecture in Norway.

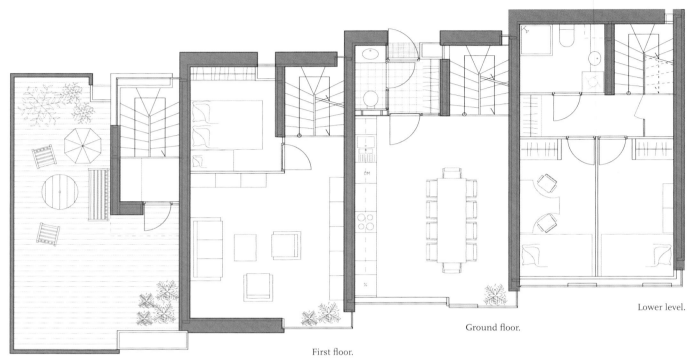

Plan, roof terrace.

First floor.

Ground floor.

Lower level.

A revolutionary housing project in Tromsø demonstrates the possibility of passive energy construction in one of the world's harshest climates.

The project is located in the Storelva neighbourhood of Kvaløya, an island area outside Tromsø in the far north of Norway. The site has a panoramic view of the fjord and the mountains. The name Storelva stems from a river that flows near the boundary of the site. The houses are fairly close to the road, but sheltered outdoor recreation areas have been established to the west and north, away from the traffic. These outdoor recreation areas also provide an effective buffer to the rushing sound of the river.

The development consists of a row of seven houses, all with a living area on three floors and a private roof terrace, where there is sun from early morning to late evening in the summer. Six of the houses have three bedrooms, kitchen/family room, living room, bathroom and additional WC. The end house facing the river has only one room on each floor, as well as a bath and WC.

The construction principle is based on an earlier project known as i-BOX, built by Steinsvik Arkitektontor in Tromsø. All of the houses, including cellars, are built of solid timber elements, with roofs insulated with rockwool. The timber structure provides effective soundproofing. Externally the buildings are covered with Norwegian heartwood pine. Carports, storerooms, bicycle sheds, a barbeque shed and a waste recycling unit are also built of solid timber elements. The heating plant, the heart of the building, is located in a stairwell on the roof. The solar collector is integrated into the south façade, where the large glass surfaces also allow a grand view. Importance is also attached to daylighting, and there is movement-controlled lighting in all rooms.

Steinsvik Arkitektkontor

PROJECT INFORMATION: Passive energy houses, Storelva.
Address: Nedre Storvollen 40 B-H, Tromsø. **Completed:** 2008. **Client:** Maurstadgruppen. **Architect:** Steinsvik Arkitektkontor. **Team:** Odd-Karl Steinsvik, Silas Steenholdt, Tina Smith Aalling, Margret Weidner, Larissa Acharya. **Project management:** Rose Marie Steinsvik. **Gross area:** 120 sq.m. per unit. **Costs ex VAT:** NOK 2 880 000 per unit (incl. site cost). **Photos:** Ravn Steinsvik

ENVIRONMENTAL INFORMATION: Estimated energy consumption: 49.5 kWh/sq.m. GBA per year. Estimated energy consumption per unit is 6000 kWh per year. **Average U-value:** 0.10 W/sq.m.K. **Ventilation:** Balanced mechanical ventilation. **Energy sources:** Solar heat collector, geothermal heat collector, heat pump.

28 ROYAL NORWEGIAN EMBASSY
KATHMANDU, NEPAL
KRISTIN JARMUND ARKITEKTER

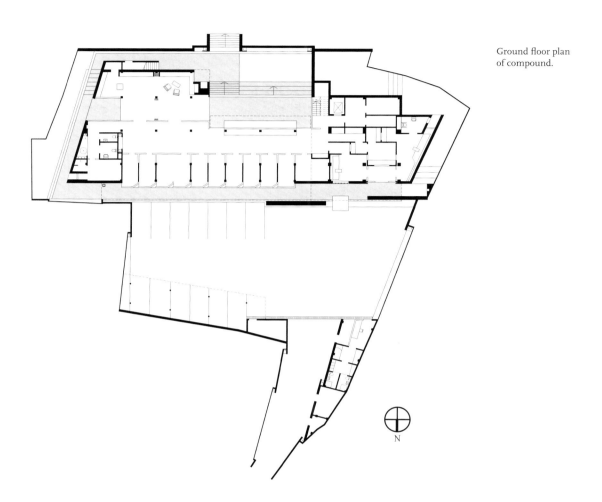

Ground floor plan
of compound.

On a hill above Kathmandu, looking out over the Himalayas, the new building for the Norwegian Embassy combines tradition and modernity.

The new Norwegian Embassy is a freestanding building in the garden of the older villa. The villa, which formerly housed the embassy, is to be demolished to make way for a new ambassador's residence. The site measures about 4000 sq.m. The design of the building and its landscape are intended to present a modest, yet up-to-date and quality-conscious image of Norway. At the same time the design and detailing should not be entirely alien to Nepalese architecture and the use of materials should reflect local building traditions.

Most of the building is on a single level and has a low profile in the landscape, apart from a small two-storey volume marking the main entrance. This gives the rooms in the upper floor a panoramic view of the Himalayas, which are reflected in a long zigzag-shaped "Himalayan window".

Natural stone of high quality has been used throughout, and shelves planted with vegetation are built into the walls. The aim is to present Norwegian culture through an open and transparent working environment, where the various rooms are divided by glass partitions. A long hallway links the offices and common rooms and opens onto a south-facing terrace. External steps, the foundation wall and the outer walls of the basement are faced with slate. The top-floor facades and the slab edges are faced with light-coloured travertine. Nepalese sesau wood has been used for pergolas, ventilation grilles and some elements of the facade. The main structure is a stiff framework of columns and beams, with free-spanning slabs of in-situ concrete, in accordance with the requirements for buildings in earthquake areas. The detailing was developed by local consultants in cooperation with Kristin Jarmund Arkitekter. Local entrepreneurs and local workmen were used. Statsbygg (The Directorate of Public Construction and Property) provided temporary accommodation for the workmen and their families for the duration of the project.

Kristin Jarmund Arkitekter

PROJECT INFORMATION: Chancery of the Royal Norwegian Embassy in Kathmandu. **Address:** Lalitpur, Kathmandu, Nepal. **Completed:** 2008. **Client:** Statsbygg – Public Construction and Property Management and the Norwegian Ministry of Foreign Affairs. **Architect:** Kristin Jarmund Arkitekter. **Team:** Kristin Jarmund, Graeme Ferguson. **Interior architect:** Linda Evensen. **Landscape architect:** Multiconsult, Seksjon 13,3, K Landskapsarkitekter. **Local consultant:** Archiplan, Kathmandu. **Gross area:** 830 sq.m. **Cost exclusive of VAT:** NOK 18 million. **Photos:** Guri Dahl and kristin Jarmund Arkitekter.

ENVIRONMENTAL INFORMATION: **Energy consumption:** Not known. **Land use:** 37 sq.m./person. **Average U-value:** Not relevant in Nepal. **Sources of energy:** Electricity from the local grid and a generator for backup. **Ventilation:** Natural ventilation, air-conditioning units for cooling and heating. **Other features:** Rain-water collection and re-use. Underground tanks have been installed to collect the rainwater, which is filtered through sand. Solar power is used to heat the water.

29 RAJIV GANDHI INTERNATIONAL AIRPORT HYDERABAD, INDIA

AVIAPLAN/NARUD STOKKE WIIG ARKITEKTER OG PLANLEGGERE, NORWAY, COWI DENMARK AND STUP CONSULTANTS, INDIA

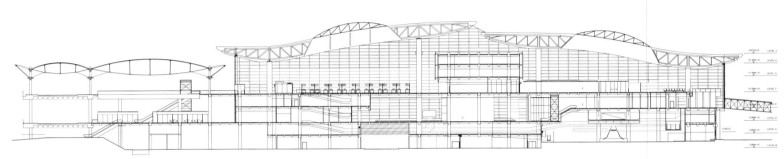

Main cross section.

Norwegian architects bring expertise and sensitivity to the development of Indian aviation. The new airport in Hyderabad combines efficiency with tradition.

The commission was to design an airport of the highest international standard with a future capacity of 40–50 million passengers a year. It was to be a gateway to India, representative of a high level of culture and technology, and to act as a locomotive for economic growth and development in the region. Hyderabad, where the airport is located, is the fifth largest city in India, with a population of approximately 5 million, and together with Bangalore it is one of the main hubs of the rapidly growing Indian IT industry.

The airport lies about 30 kilometres outside the city centre, and covers an area of approximately 25 square kilometres. The site is a gently rolling agricultural landscape with palms, fruit trees, rice fields and small rocky knolls. Two long ridges enclosing a shallow valley form a natural framework for the development. One of the main principles of the project was flexibility and the potential for rapid growth in capacity, and the airport has expanded rapidly.

Part of the challenge was to give the airport a distinct identity and a sense of place – it was to say: This is India! This is Hyderabad!

Based on a systematic approach to the environment, the place and the mood, the architects achieved diversity in the form of:

– A modern, efficient and attractive terminal building adapted to local climatic conditions and available building technology,
– A spacious Airport Village for meeters and greeters, with shops, services and restaurants, protected from the sun and rain by a fabric roof structure, in front of the terminal building,
– A large shady park beyond the Airport Village, with seating and access to parking, bus terminal, hotels, etc.

The technological solutions were adapted to what was technically and financially feasible, and energy and the environment were emphasised throughout the planning and construction processes. The shape of the roof has been specifically designed to cope with the sun, and double glazing and insulation in the walls and roof reduce the need for artificial cooling. The energy-saving measures have earned the building a high LEED rating. The subcontractors came from many different countries but the workforce was mainly Indian. The building process seemed at times to be somewhat chaotic, since century-old building traditions were being combined with highly sophisticated modern building technology. The airport was built over a 3.5-year period by 7000 workers.

Aviaplan

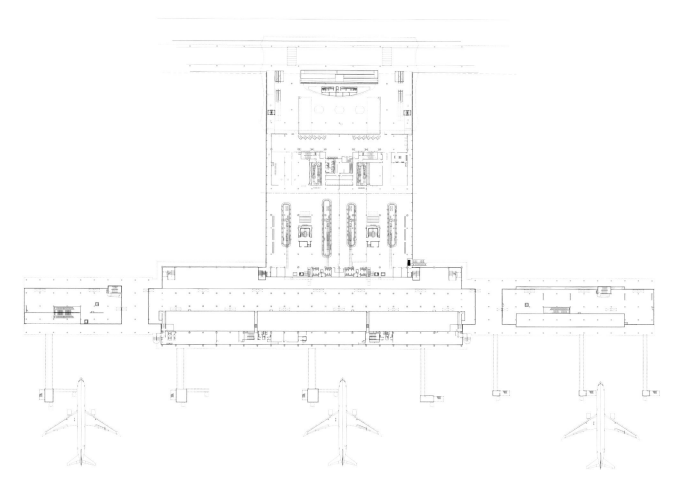

Entrance level plan.

PROJECT INFORMATION: Rajiv Gandhi International Airport. **Address:** Hyderabad, Andhra Pradesh, India. **Completed:** 2008. **Client:** GHIAL (GMR Hyderabad International Airport Limited). **Architect:** Aviaplan/Narud Stokke Wiig Arkitekter og Planleggere in cooperation with COWI, Denmark, and STUP Consultants, India. **Team:** Gudmund Stokke (project leader), Geoffrey Clark, Christian Henriksen, Pål Laurantzon, Roald Sand, Ole Tørklep, Tom Holtmann. Astrid Frøvig, interior architect; Jostein Bjørbekk of Bjørbekk & Lindheim, landscape architect. **Detail design:** Integrated Design Associates Hong Kong, under the supervision of Winston Schu of NSW. **Landscape architect:** Belt Collins International, Singapore. **Consultants:** COWI, Arup, Hong Kong. **Gross area:** 117 000 sq.m. **Cost exclusive of VAT:** approx. NOK 3 500 million. **Photos:** Somashekar D. P.

ENVIRONMENTAL INFORMATION: The project was awarded the LEED Silver Certificate for features such as the use of local materials, energy optimisation and waste management (recovery and composting), re-use of grey water (recycling and watering of outside areas) and rain-water harvesting. **Ventilation:** Mechanical.

30 PREIKESTOLEN MOUNTAIN LODGE JØRPELAND

HELEN & HARD

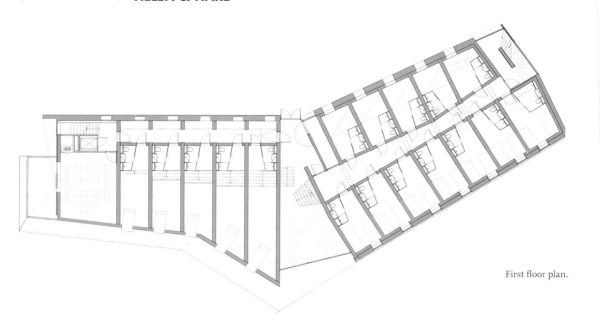

First floor plan.

The new mountain lodge at Preikestolen takes timber construction one step further, combining international technology and local craftsmanship.

With approximately 120 000 visitors each year, the rock formation Preikestolen is one of Norway's most popular tourist destinations. Stavanger Trekking Association had long toyed with the idea of a new building to serve the increasing numbers of tourists. There was already a lodge on the site, built in 1949, but it had become too small. Moreover, many tourists want something better than bunk beds and a shared bathroom in the corridor. The Trekking Association wanted to provide for the new needs with a new facility, but still wished to retain some of the unpretentiousness that is typical of Norwegian mountain lodges. In 2004, they announced a local architecture competition, which was won by Helen & Hard.

The design of the building volume reflects the sweep of the landscape and the formations of the terrain. The building has been placed around a crag. Heights and roof gradients have been adapted and tuned to match the sheer mountainsides to the north-east and the more gentle ridges to the west. The main structure consists of 15 double, prefabricated solid timber ribs placed 2.8 metres apart and cut through to form the large common rooms on the first floor. The ribs form the partitions between the guest rooms, and provide intimate seating booths along the façade of the restaurant.

In the bedroom area, floor decks have been hung between the wall ribs. The bathrooms have been constructed with three glass walls and one wooden wall. All walls carrying service installations are alike. All tradesmen were able to work with open installations on the solid timber wall, and the installations were subsequently clad with glass. The whole structure is detailed so that the thick wood walls are diffusive. The hygroscopic properties of the solid timber slabs avoids the need for vapour barriers, and windproofing and waterproofing are solved by means of waxed fibreboards. The saddle roofs have a double underlay with air circulation and ventilation openings at the top and along all ridges. In the flattest areas of the roof, an additional layer of metal sheeting has been inserted between the fibre board and ceiling boards. The building has been clad on the outside with heartwood pine and treated with iron vitriol. All materials are toxin- and emission free. Heating is water-borne via circuits under the slate floor, fed from a heat pump in the Refsvatnet lake.

Local building- and craft traditions formed the starting point for the design and selection of interior elements. Wood basketwork is used on cupboard fronts and partition walls in the restaurant. Straw wallpaper on the ceiling is part of a sound absorbent layer. Chairs and benches have been made by a former ski manufacturer, while furniture covers have been specially made by a local weaver.

Preikestolen Mountain Lodge is a Norwegian Wood project. Norwegian Wood was an important part of Stavanger European Culture Capital 2008, organised by NAL | Ecobox and Stavanger Municipality. The projects gave particularly high priority to ecology and sustainability, and were required to meet stringent criteria with regard to innovative use of wood, environmentally friendly use of materials, low energy consumption and universal design.

Helen & Hard

PROJECT INFORMATION: **Name:** Preikestolen Mountain Lodge. **Adress:** Preikestolveien 521, Jørpeland. **Completed:** 2008. **Architects:** Helen & Hard. **Team:** Siv Helen Stangeland, Reinhard Kropf, Dag Strass. **Interior:** Helen & Hard. **Landscape:** Helen & Hard. **Photos:** Jiri Havran.

ENVIRONMENTAL INFORMATION: **Energy consumption:** 110 kWh/sq.m. per year. **Average U-values (W/kvm)K:** Walls/Roof: 0, 12, ground: 0,9, windows: 0, 7 and 1,1. **Energy sources:** Ground water heat exchange from water to water heat pump, supplemented by logburner. **Ventilation:** Balanced mechanical ventilation with heat recovery.

PERFORMATIVE FREEDOM

INTERVIEW | **REINHARD KROPF, PARTNER, HELEN & HARD**
HELLE BENEDICTE BERG

"Evocative and sensual" is how the duo Helen & Hard describe the structure they have created for the World Exposition in Shanghai 2010. The Stavanger based office, founded by Siv Helene Stangeland and Reinhard Kropf, has a lot of experience of combining playfulness with responsibility, and they have mastered the balance between the conscious and the apparently unrestrained. Helle Benedicte Berg spoke to Reinhard Kropf about the challenges of creating innovative and at the same time sustainable architecture - for such a super-scale commercial event as the Expo.

REINHARD KROPF: Originally we weren't interested in competing for the Norwegian Expo pavilion. That is, until we heard that the theme would be "Better City. Better Life", and that it revolved around sustainable urban development and urbanisation. It was a creative challenge to explore how such a contribution, where enormous resources are spent just to be thrown away afterwards, also

has the possibility to be sustainable and meaningful for a longer period of time.

HELLE BENEDICTE BERG: Which would seem to be a contradiction?
RK: It was clear to us from the outset that the life of the pavilion after the Expo was the most important form-generating force in this project. Or more precisely: How the reuse may mirror what Norway would like to convey in such a setting; and simultaneously express a concrete spatial and structural idea. In short, this structural idea consists of fifteen "trees" built of Norwegian laminated wood and Chinese bamboo, which together form the spatial arena of the pavilion. Each tree can easily be flat-packed into a container and reerected elsewehere after the Expo. The "roots" of the trees make up the exhibition, which are woven together to make an organic experience landscape. The treetops are made with a membrane ceiling, which is divided into fifteen four-point sails.

HBB: What possibilities did the context provide? The site and the area along the Huang-pu River in the centre of Shanghai? We have heard how traditional homesteads were demolished and people relocated for the benefit of the Expo constructions?
RK: From the outset, we were interested in understanding the history of the Expo site. We did some preliminary investigations into the relocation projects where tens of thousands of families were relocated to new housing areas outside Shanghai. China's relocation policy is complex and in our view radical, and it is difficult to understand it from a European point of view, which is more protective of the individual. Cultural differences aside, it appears that many people find that these new housing projects lack common areas, areas for play and recreation. So this need became the conceptual starting point for our development of the pavilion. Our original idea was that it would be relocated and reused as park installations and playgrounds in the new

"THE FOREST HAS BEEN OUR INSPIRATION AT A SUPERIOR LEVEL IN THIS PROJECT BECAUSE IT IS A FANTASTIC PLAYGROUND FOR PHYSICAL ACTIVITY, EXPLORATION, SOCIAL AND ASSOCIATIVE PLAY. IT WAS EXACTLY THIS PERFORMATIVE FREEDOM THAT WE WANTED IN THE PAVILION".

housing areas. In hindsight we see that this, in its original form, was naïve, and not possible to realise in such a short time frame. But the idea created a meaningful driving force that was essential for the development of the project. The result of this early contextual study is still embodied in the pavilion – in the abundance of "trees" in a park landscape that can be easily deconstructed, moved, reconstructed and adjusted to fit new places and activities.

HBB: Your practice has previously expressed that you aim to explore the potential for sustainability and resource management in each of your projects. How has that been realised here?
RK: Apart from our conscious use of resources as a consequence of the short-lived Expo event, we asked some more general questions in the competition phase, related to how Norway could contribute to the theme "Better City. Better Life". We recruited a resource group of people with a knowledge of and grounding in Chinese society. After a few workshops at Tou Scene in Stavanger,

collaboration with these institutions will continue. Another early intention was to build the trees using a new product called Glue-bam, i.e. glue laminated bamboo. We started a collaboration with the product patent-owner. But this part of the project unfortunately failed, as glue-bam has yet to become an approved building material in China. We still used bamboo as the building material for all the secondary parts of the trees, though; in the roots that make up the exhibition and the "landscape of perception" and in the lining of the branches that conceal all the technical installations. We have also collaborated closely with the Chinese practice SHZF, especially in the detailed design and follow-up phase. And with the exception of the main structure for the trees, the entire pavilion is produced in China.

HBB: This is a commercial project – Shanghai Expo is being compared to the Olympic games in Beijing. How has this influenced your architectural expression?

tion behind the Expo-pavilion?
RK: We have wanted to weave different elements together into a new evocative and perceptible landscape. In the office we called it "the Expo garden". Each "tree" combines construction, skin, infrastructure, technology, exhibition and interior. The trees are grouped together in an interpretation of four characteristic Norwegian landscapes: Coast, forest, fjord and the Arctic. These are also thematically emphasised in films etc. Through this interweaving we want to express some of the multifaceted relationships between nature, culture and commercial activities in Norwegian society. The intention is that these aspects inspire different behaviour and perceptions; from sensuous play, social life and intellectual stimuli to pure entertainment without it becoming a cacophony of impressions, or too obvious or predictable.

HBB: You say you want the architecture to counteract boredom. How has Shanghai and China been an inspiration in that regard?

"IT WAS A CREATIVE CHALLENGE TO EXPLORE HOW SUCH A CONTRIBUTION, WHERE ENORMOUS RESOURCES ARE SPENT JUST TO BE THROWN AWAY AFTERWARDS, ALSO HAS THE POSSIBILITY TO BE SUSTAINABLE AND MEANINGFUL FOR A LONGER PERIOD OF TIME."

we concluded that Norway's contribution should be to emphasise recreation areas, parks and meeting points in the city through open and democratic processes. The exhibition in the pavilion is based on these ideas. Moreover, the use of wood in the pavilion is environmentally friendly. We believe that there is potential for a transfer of knowledge to China in this area of technology.

HBB: To what degree have you employed local people and resources?
RK: Various organisations, groups and individuals have become involved in the work on the reuse of the structures. We have held workshops with students from GAFA in Guangzhou and from the Tongji University of Shanghai on how the trees may be reused. The results were presented in Guangzhou and Shanghai in November, and we are hoping that the

RK: Yes, it is a commercial project, but the development process has mainly been driven by bureaucratic forces. This has been a great challenge and frustrating at times; especially in view of the short deadlines we have had. But it is exactly this impossible situation – with various partners involved, cultural differences, the commercial spectacle on the one hand and Expo theme on the other – that has also been like an inspiring beehive. From the outset we were aware that we were skating on thin ice and that we needed a robust and flexible concept that could endure all the troubles along the way. With this in mind, we developed these fifteen trees that contain "everything", a visible and entertaining pavilion which still clearly conveys an important message.

HBB: You are ambitious. In the context of your architecture, what is the inten-

RK: A playful expression in itself is not important to us. Some of our projects have a playful expression because they mirror playful processes and experiments, and because they invite people to different forms of play. These are projects like "Base Camp", the adventure facilities for children and youngsters by the Preikestolen Mountain Lodge, the Geopark in Stavanger, where the main theme is the re-use of material from the oil industry, or the Expo pavilion. In case of the pavilion, the forest has been our inspiration at a basic level in the project, because the forest is a fantastic playground for physical activity, exploration, social and associative play. It was exactly this performative freedom that we wanted in the pavilion. During the process we realised that with 15 000 visitors per day, the interaction between the visitors and the pavilion needed to be controlled.

Above: From Preikestolen Mountain Lodge, treetop sleepout retreats for children and youngsters, 2009. Right: Restaurant Stim, Stavanger, 2004. Decorations by Hildegard Håheim (ceiling), Randy Naylor (bar).

PHOTO: HELEN & HARD, EMILE ASHLEY

At the same time the intention was that the associations that the pavilion inspires would move freely: from a forest to a Chinese dragon to a landscape of snow, to a covered market, and so on.

HBB: Helen & Hard are known for working closely with their clients and for making use of different media in their work processes. You shoot films, write stories, do interviews. What has your approach been here, in that you have had to relate to a different language, a different culture, other social norms and conventions?

RK: The cultural differences became a serious challenge that we had not foreseen from the outset. Luckily, we have a Chinese employee in our practice who helped out a lot. Innovation Norway also recruited a Chinese resource group who evaluated the pavilion and the exhibition throughout the process, which proved to be useful and informative. Due to the many participants and variables in the design process, we fixed conditions at the micro- and meso levels which allow for a certain degree of self-organisation within a clearly established language. The entire exhibition landscape, for instance, is made of prefabricated bamboo boards that are cut and put together according to various principles within each landscape. Regardless of whether the landscape needs to be changed, we have established an overall unity in the expression.

HBB: In the World Expo in Brussels in 1958, Sverre Fehn represented Norway with a pavilion in Norwegian laminated wood. You have called architects like Sverre Fehn and Christian Norberg-Schulz the "Norwegian purists of modernism". Do you think such "Norwegianness" helps or hinders the understanding of your work?

RK: That quote is from a conversation about Sverre Fehn's and Christian Norberg-Schulz' perception of a predefined and pure relation between the architecture and a cultural, geographic and landscape context. This relation partly has categorical and essentialist traits that are not very suitable for the development of projects in changing and culturally complex environments. We perceived Sverre Fehn's and Norberg-Schulz' teaching as focusing on an increased sensibility towards what is significant and essential in a situation, articulated in a poetic language that may be moulded into clear structures, material authenticity and meaningful architectonic motives. In such work, context is understood in more purist norms, categories and essences rather than as a relational creation, an interwoven topology of situational circumstances.

HBB: I suppose you needed a more open approach for the project in Shanghai. What does Norway and China have to offer each other, in the current architectural situation?

RK: I am sure there is potential for exchange. However, the political conditions and the scale of Norwegian and Chinese architectural projects are so different that it is difficult to point out concrete possibilities for transfer of knowledge and professional exchange. We have experienced that the precondition for collaboration lies in a clear and specialized competence needed in the Chinese market. Of course they also shop for European stars.

HBB: Can you imagine doing any more projects in China?

RK: We would like to do an environmentally friendly housing project or a restoration project. It would be interesting to transform many of the old villages that are being demolished in Shanghai into new neighbourhoods. And we still hope to be able to work on the reuse of the fifteen trees.

Helle Benedicte Berg

Expo 2010 Shanghai is the first World Fair to adopt sustainable urban development as its theme: "Better City – Better Life". The concept of the Norwegian pavilion, "Powered by Nature", directly engages this challenge, emphasising several aspects of sustainability.

The explosive urbanization that China is experiencing calls for an increased sensibility and consideration for both natural and human resources. The pavilion contributes to these issues with an architecture that facilitates social sustainability, healthy public recreational areas and environmentally friendly urban structures and infrastructures. The pavilion consists of 15 "trees", prefabricated in timber, which create a sensory and multifunctional "forest".

Each tree combines structure, skin, infrastructure (air-conditioning, water- and energy supply, lighting etc.), furniture, exhibition, playground and information display. The "tree" structure allows each component to be autonomous or combined with others. After the Expo, each of the "trees" can be easily dismantled and relocated elsewhere, to serve a number of uses: a park installation, playground, social meeting place etc.

The main structure is made from laminated timber. Each "tree" consists of a fabric roof, four "branches", a "trunk" and "roots". The components can be packed flat to make optimal use of space and transportation. A recently developed Chinese timber product, GluBam – Glue-laminated Bamboo, is used for secondary structures, the exhibitions and most of the surfaces in the pavilion. The roof of the pavilion is a four point membrane construction. The fabric shades against direct sunlight while admitting diffused light, thus saving energy for interior lighting.

The roots of the trees are shaped to give assosiations to four characteristic Norwegian landscapes: the coast, the forest, the fjords and the Arctic. The spatial characteristics and intrinsic qualities of these landscapes are the foundation of the design in the interior zones of the pavilion.

Helen & Hard

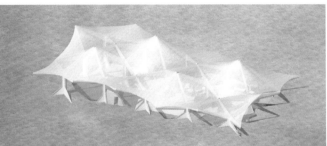

After the Expo, the pavilon "trees" can be dismantled and reused for different functions around the city if Shanghai.

ILLUSTRATIONS: HELEN & HARD

PROJECT INFORMATION: Norway – Powered by Nature. **Architect:** Helen & Hard. **Team:** Siv Helene Stangelang and Reinhard Kropf, Moritz Groba, Randi H. Augenstein, Ute Schmidt, Mu Wei, Paco Puga Ortiz. **Interior:** Helen & Hard. **Gross area:** 1525 sq.m. **Photos:** Helen & Hard.

ENVIRONMENTAL INFORMATION: Materials: Timber, GluBam – glue-laminated bamboo. **Energy sources:** Solar panels, water collection and adjustable air vents are all integrated into the architecture and part of the exhibition. Rainwater will be collected on the pavilion roof and purified. The purification technology is made visible and understandable to the public, who is invited to sip cooled, clean water from open taps. **Ventilation:** Natural (chimney effect plus wind).

MOJAVE ASTER
Machaeranthera Tortifolia
Habitat : S. California, Arizona, Utah

California City
HOLIDAY INN
By The Lake

Approaching Galileo Hill   Approaching the First Community

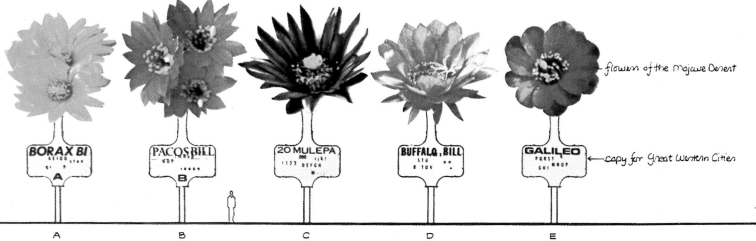

BORAX BI

PACOS BILL

20 MULEPA

BUFFALO BILL

GALILEO

flowers of the Mojave Desert

copy for Great Western Cities

A   B   C   D   E

THE PROBLEM OF AESTHETICS

Architecture is said to be an "aesthetic discipline". But what does the term 'aesthetic' actually mean? Is it a neutral concept, unfettered by ideology, or does it actually limit the development of an architectural debate that is becoming more and more pressing, namely the value of ethics in architecture?

ESSAY | **MARI HVATTUM**
Professor at the Oslo School of Architecture and Design

'Aesthetics' has long been a mantra in Norwegian public debate. We encounter the word in newspaper columns and government reports, in political speeches promising more 'aesthetic quality' and in the common dirge of journalists and architects over the 'aesthetic decline' of the public sphere. Architecture is said to be an 'aesthetic discipline', and should as such be grouped together with the other 'aesthetic subjects' in school curricula. What the term 'aesthetics' actually *means* is less clear. As used in everyday language, the word seems to apply mainly to visual quality: to whether things are ugly or beautiful. Is 'aesthetics' synonymous with visual quality? And if so, is it visual quality that is the criterion for good architecture? A closer examination of the term aesthetics may prompt a discussion of the means and aims of architecture today – a discussion worth keeping alive.

If the concept of aesthetics is unclear in Norwegian public debate, the matter is certainly made no clearer by the academic literature. 'Aesthetics' has been assigned a number of meanings. Philosophers define it as "the study of aesthetic objects and [...] subjective aesthetic experience", while artists and art theorists speak about 'aesthetic value' in the sense of artistic quality.[1] Whether one defines aesthetics as art theory or as a criterion for artistic quality, however, it is mostly taken for granted that aesthetics in itself is a neutral, non-ideological concept, and that one can safely discuss 'Plato's aesthetics' or the 'aesthetic qualities' of Snøhetta's Opera building in Oslo, without getting tangled in a terminological mess.

Bearing this apparently harmless concept in mind, it may come as a surprise that the term aesthetics has itself in recent times been subjected to considerable criticism. The German philosopher Hans-Georg Gadamer refers to aesthetics as a "dubious" concept, and views the emergence of modern aesthetics as symptomatic of a deep cultural crisis.[2] Martin Heidegger presents the even more radical view that great art came to an end at the moment in history when aesthetics achieved its greatest possible height.[3] Aesthetics, then, is perhaps not such an innocent designation of either art theory or artistic value,

but a concept that, in itself, expresses a specific view of art. What does this view entail and how can it be said to have bearing upon architecture?

What does 'aesthetics' mean?
The word 'aesthetics' is derived from the Greek 'aisthesis', and pertains to 'things perceptible by the senses'. For the Greeks, however, the word had little to do with art. Art was primarily a religious concern; a representation of a higher order. Not until the early part of the 18th century did aesthetics in the modern sense come into being, named by the German philosopher Alexander Gottlieb Baumgarten.[4] Baumgarten's undertaking was simple. In an intellectual climate dominated by Descartes' rationalism, sensate experience was under threat. Baumgarten's project, then, was a rescue operation aimed to render sensate experience legitimate as an independant domain of knowledge. This domain was given the name *aesthetics*; an autonomous science with sensate experience – including the experience of art – as its subject matter. Aesthetics, however, was not on a level with reason; it was a *'gnosologia inferior'*, exhorted Baumgarten – an inferior branch of knowledge, humbly subordinated to pure reason. Aesthetics is reason's 'younger sister', explained Baumgarten, and, like all women, she is pleasant to have around the house although she mainly occupies herself with trivialities. Baumgarten's understanding of sense perception as an inferior form of knowledge involved a radical breach with a premodern tradition, where perception was always seen to be a medium for representation of truth, and as such not categorically separate from reason. Baumgarten and modern aesthetics put an end to this. Sense and sensibility were for the first time regarded as incompatible faculties, alternative and competing conceptions of reality. Baumgarten's aesthetics was further pursued by both rationalist and romantic thinkers during the eighteenth and nineteenth centuries, by Kant, and by Hegel, who was the first to view aesthetics as simply a philosophy of art. In Hegel's view, art does not attain perfection until its content is totally absorbed by its form, that is to say when

it can be appraised on the basis of stringent formal criteria, as an autonomous work, without regard to utility value or other contextual considerations.[5]

The insistence on autonomy, *art for art's sake,* has been one of the most important characteristics of modern aesthetics. The position opens up two seemingly contradictory avenues for art. Isolated from its original social and epistemological context, art could on the one hand be elevated to an alternative reality or, on the other hand be banished as irrelevant decoration. The former view was favoured in the Romantic period, when art was viewed as an 'aesthetic world' (Schiller), an escape from the 'deadly' rationalism of the Enlightenment. The latter view prevailed in Positivist thinking of the 19th and 20th centuries, asserting the need for the absolute subjection of art to reason. These apparently contradictory trends are however two sides of the same coin. Whether elevated or banished, the modern insistence on autonomy entails a fundamental separation of art from other areas of society. Modern aesthetics reduces art to an isolated work which, disconnected from the world, can be interpreted on the basis of its own formal criteria.

Gadamer has called this isolation 'aesthetic differentiation' [*ästhetische Unterscheidung*], and views it as one of the most problematic aspects of modern thinking. As he writes:

"Aesthetic experience is directed towards what is supposed to be the work proper – what it ignores are the extra-aesthetic elements that cling to it, such as purpose, function, the significance of its content [...] By disregarding everything in which a work is rooted (its original context of life, and the religious or secular function that gave it significance), it becomes visible as the 'pure work of art'. [...] Thus through "aesthetic differentiation" the work loses its place and the world to which it belongs insofar as it belongs instead to aesthetic consciousness"[6]

This is the paradox of the modern aesthetics. Conceived as a defence of sensate experience, aesthetics contributed instead to the isolation and decontextualisation of art and sensation alike. Even when the aesthetic experience is elevated as an alternative reality and cultivated as an aesthetic refuge, as did the Romantics, this fragmentation is confirmed rather than disproved. Modern aesthetics divests art of its ancient role as embodied meaning and banishes it to the splendid isolation of the museum.

Aesthetics, architecture, and human action

'Aesthetics', then, is far from a neutral designation of either art theory or artistic value. The term expresses a very specific view of art, a view whereby art is reduced to 'works', and whereby its social, historical and ideological context is ignored. Such a narrowing of the interpretation of the art-work is particularly problematic for architecture whose multiple entanglements with context, use, function and meaning are so profound. An aesthetic understanding of architecture will inevitably be one that renders architecture into a matter of visual effect – a kind of Venturi'an *"decorated shed"*. The philosopher Karsten

Harries warns against such an aesthetic understanding of architecture in the book *The Ethical Function of Architecture*. "It is [...] hardly surprising," writes Harries, "that with the rise of the aesthetic approach in the eighteenth century, architecture should have entered a period of uncertainty and crisis from which it has still not emerged."[7] By viewing architecture as a primarily aesthetic phenomenon, we are in danger of ignoring its ethical dimension. We forget, in other words, the complex interpretation of human actions and history which are embodied in any building and any town. To be sure, the visual appearance of towns and buildings are part of this hermeneutic work. But only a part. And as long as 'aesthetic quality' remains the undisputed ideal for architecture, it will be difficult to discover the rest.

We undoubtedly need terms that grasp the beauty and quality of our environment and enable us to defend such values in political debates as well as in everyday discussions. The question, however, is whether 'aesthetics' is such a term. Language is not innocent. By using the apparently positively charged concept of aesthetics as an undebatable ideal for architecture, we are in danger of reducing both the meaning and the significance of the built environment, ultimately turning architectural debate into a quarrel about ugly vs nice. By unanimously focusing on the 'aesthetic aspect' of architecture, we are in danger of assuming that *this* is what architecture is all about. I maintain that this is not the case. Architecture is not primarily a visual art, but an art whose objective is to accommodate and facilitate human action. Architecture is engaged in a complex organisational interpretation of our lives in form and space. This is a task beyond aesthetics. It is a task that is more closely associated with ethics, as a question of how one accommodates that which at any given time is perceived as the good life. Perhaps well-meaning government reports should concern themselves more with what architecture *does*, and less with the way it looks.

Mari Hvattum

Mari Hvattum is Professor at the institute of Form, Theory and History at the Oslo School of Architecture and Design.

NOTES
1 Wladyslaw Tatarkiewicz, *History of Aesthetics*, vol.1. Den Haag: Mouton 1970–74. Introduction.
2 Hans-Georg Gadamer, *Truth and Method*, London: Sheed & Ward 1989, Part I, chp 3 (A).
3 Martin Heidegger, *Nietzsche* vol.1, translated by D. Farrell Krell, New York: Routledge & Kegan, 1979, chapter 13.
4 *Meditationes philosophicae de nonnullis ad poema pertinentibus.* English translation: *Reflections on Poetry.* K. Aschenbrenner & W. B. Holther. University of California Press 1954
5 *Vorlesungen über die Asthetik* (1818-29).
6 Gadamer *op.cit.* pp. 85-87.
7 Karsten Harries, *The Ethical Function of Architecture*, Cambridge Mass.: MIT Press 1997. p. 26.

Illustration p. 138: Roadsigns for Twenty Mule Team Parkway. From *Learning from Las Vegas*, Robert Venturi, Denise Scott Brown and Steven Izenour, 1972. Facing page: Wallpaper. From *Der Tapetenfabrikant Johann Christian Arnold, 1758-1842*, Sabine Trümmler. Sparkasse Kassel/Staatliche Museen Kassel 1998.

INDEX

BUILDINGS